INSIDE PANDORA

Jesper Nielsen

As told to philosopher, Carsten Graff

INSIDE PANDORA

Jesper Nielsen

As told to philosopher, Carsten Graff

Inside Pandora

Copyright © 2014 StemningsHotellet
First edition, first printing 2014
Cover art: Carsten Valentin
Published by StemningsHotellet, Tjornevej 22,
DK-2800 Lyngby, Denmark
Printed by CPI books GmbH
ISBN 978-87-996018-2-0

Endless Jewelry

www.endlessjewelry.eu
www.endlessjewelry.us
www.facebook.com/endlessjewelry

Other publications by Carsten Graff

Conversations with an Oak Tree, 2012
A former computer nerd on why computers save neither
time nor money.

Dreamcatcher, 2012
A personal account of multilevel marketing told by one the
world's top practitioners.

Amazon.com

TABLE OF CONTENTS

Carsten's preface

The business world is not one of my big passions, but I have to admit I was completely hooked the moment I first heard Jesper's story. Northern European culture is incredibly traditional with a large complex of rules for what personal fulfillment and commercial success should look like and what methods for attaining them are acceptable. These rules are an ingrained part of the social fabric. We are told that we must be available by phone, dress a certain way, have the right education, use management or life coaches, attend training seminars in personal development, and make "friends" with people on Facebook. When I first met Jesper, I realized that he had reached the absolute pinnacle of the business world and had done so ignoring those rules and without doing any of the things considered mandatory in the business world. Jesper does not have a formal education; he does not wear jackets or neckties; he only uses the phone when talking with his family; and would never dream of using a coach or attend personal development seminars. He has no interest in his competitors; he hires people without looking at their résumés; and drafting advanced business plans has no place in his universe. In many ways, he is living evidence that almost everything that is being preached in business school and textbooks can sometimes be a huge impediment to a successful career. This made me perk up my ears. I wanted to hear more about his life and his work and explore this challenge to conventional thinking, and therefore, I decided to interview him a couple of hours at a time to hear more about his incredible story.

All the books I have written have been about believing in and trusting simplicity, about daring to be authentic, and about exploring the energy that arises between people bold enough to be honest. I have primarily based my work on my own experiences; this time, however, it gave me great pleasure to write about someone else's experiences. Personally, I find Jesper's approach to career and business to be a breath of fresh air, and it is a true delight for me to be a position to blow some of that fresh air into a culture that in many ways seems stultified and rigid in its beliefs about what can or cannot be done. Most people have a tendency to overthink things so much that it prevents them from accomplishing the simplest things. In many ways, Jesper's philosophy is almost frighteningly simple—and once you have heard his story and unique perspective, it is pretty hard to argue that simple does not work.

Carsten Graff
carstengraff@gmail.com
www.carstengraff.dk

In Jesper's Words

Warming Up

Jesper introduces his universe

In 2004, I started out in Germany as a reseller of jewelry made by the company, Pandora. Back then, I had no money, knew nothing about jewelry, and spoke no German. Six years later, I sold that same company, now populated by 500 employees, offices in six countries, and sales, during that last year, of nearly $270 million. Naturally, the obvious question is how do you manage to grow a business at such a rate. I have often been asked if I have a recipe for this kind of growth, any specific training or education, or special knowledge. My answer: If you want to go far, recipes, academic programs, training, and special knowledge can prove to be more of a burden than a benefit. Sure, knowledge can be excellent. But in business, if we are talking about the kind of knowledge you get from reading the same books as everyone else—well, frankly, that is not worth much. If you want to create something unique, your thought processes must be unique and you must be unique. To put it differently, you need to go beyond known boundaries and head off in new directions. We all know how to read books, follow a recipe, or create a spreadsheet. Doing something that no one else has thought of and that you will not find in any books, *that* requires courage. And that is perhaps one of the greatest gifts I have been given—that is what has allowed me to produce results on the scale that I have.

You will *not* find any of the steps I took to supercharge my business in textbooks. If you are the well-adjusted, well-groomed corporate type who always follows the rules and does exactly what he is told, you will have a hard time understanding my mindset. In a culture where tradition tells you that formal training or education can help you do or be almost anything, you often forget that what creates results in groups is not about theory or book learning but about energy and gut feeling. Once you learn how to channel your energy and listen to that gut feeling, you are free to create relationships and interactions between people; bonds that help them perform almost without limits. With that, you will be well-equipped to embark on your own extraordinary business adventure and hopefully see your own sales go through the roof. It is about shifting your focus away from the rules that limit you; it is about being willing to go to unexplored corners of the world map; it is about doing things never tried before.

The activities I come up with to grow my business I generally call my "stunts." What do I mean by "stunt"? A stunt is a movement or an activity that seems dangerous or peculiar to others. A stunt tends to attract attention because it arouses an inner desire for freedom in people stuck in the mud of inertia. This does not mean that the first time you get on a motorbike you should kid yourself into thinking that you can jump over 32 cars and land safely on the other side. No, in order to perform stunts, you need to have a sense of your surroundings and the courage to pursue the impossible—and you need to trust your gut instinct.

What I want to do with this book is to let you share my outlook on things, my experiences, my motives and motivations, but also to let you in on some of my major stunts—how and why they came about and what impact they ultimately had on my business.

/Jesper

Stunt No. 1

Go-giver

On good deeds and business success as a byproduct

A go-getter is highly ambitious person with razor-sharp elbows who will do anything to get ahead. Many would probably say that this description fits my profile pretty accurately, but that is not at all the case. A while back, I was on an airplane reading a book in which the author had coined the term "go-giver." Go-givers are individuals to whom business performance is merely a byproduct of the good deeds they do in their daily lives. That label fits me to a tee: I have always felt passionately about giving, and then I have the privilege of seeing people use and take pleasure in what I give them.

Many years before my business adventure started in earnest, I was working at a gas station mart. At the cash register, I would always give myself this little mission: Make sure everyone who enters leaves the store with a smile. I had that particular twinkle in my eye and could get away with saying pretty much anything to my customers. In fact, there is nothing better that entering a store and encountering someone cheerfully just *giving* you something—a thoughtful person who knows what he or she is doing and who just *loves* to provide great service. At the gas station, I learned that all customers have different needs, and that means that great service can never—must never—become routine, mechanical, or methodical. Everyone knows that it is not difficult to give someone a compliment and then get them to say: "You, too!" The real challenge is to create a situation where both parties actually *believe* what they are saying. If you want to have others speak from the heart and mean what they say, you must be ready to do the same. When that happens, it is no longer a matter of a commercial transaction, but it is about sincere people creating a space for mutual honesty. If you are going to succeed in a commercial transaction that makes customers happy, you must surrender yourself to a state where you give what you have while also letting go of all your expectations for a particular outcome. Every time you succeed in doing this, energy is being generated. And the greater this energy, the farther your customers will be willing to travel and return to perform the same transaction again. In order to succeed with your business, you must reach a place where you can do good deeds without hidden agendas—and if you can do that, you can characterize yourself as a go-giver.

You can be a go-giver working at a gas station mart, teaching English to kids, leading a sports team to the playoffs, or leading an international billion-dollar enterprise. In principle, where you are and what you do for a living are irrelevant. The energy you are looking to generate is the same; it is the scale that is very different.

As my business grew, I decided to create a platform from which I could practice go-giver activities to business connections, customers, and employees. One of my ideas was to create a luxury resort on the Spanish island of Mallorca. My business was named the KASI Group, so my resort became KASI House. The objective was to invite people to a place where I could give them an unbelievable experience. The house, some 6,500 square feet, is located on a mountain, exquisitely luxurious, with access to my so-called "boat." The boat was an Astondoa 82 super yacht with a fly bridge, Jacuzzi, and barbecue, 12 beds, and room for between 40 and 50 people to party and cook. In the garage: a Bentley, a Lamborghini, and a McLaren. When guests arrived, I would nonchalantly tell them that the keys for the cars and the boat were on the counter and then let them loose. I had a different place nearby where I lived with my family. But when I had guests at the KASI House, they all felt like they were truly in my home—even though they knew that I had a private residence elsewhere.

The KASI House served as a place where future business partners would get an eye-opener, where an employee would have an unforgettable vacation with his or her family, or where business connections could unwind or meet up. I would set aside 12 weeks a year for my top-performing employees. For those stays, a central part of my philosophy was that everything would be uncomplicated and immediate. If you are getting a prize or a reward, you should not have to wait until next year to get it, or six months, or even three months. As soon as the winner was announced, it was all about having that person sent to the KASI House within 14 days and, preferably, with their spouse and children. Upon arrival, I made sure they were treated like absolute royalty. This meant having a crew ready to tend to their every whim and desire. The champagne was put on ice, toys purchased for the kids, and tables were set, seeing to every little detail, with seating cards for all guests—spelled correctly. Once an employee sees that *that* is how you treat them, that *that* is your level of commitment to and interest in their well-being, that employee will go through hell and high water for you.

Once they return, they will give their all at work. And if the spouse or significant other had joined them, that spouse or partner will be quite a bit more accepting of a few extra hours of work once in a while. Apart from my constant pampering of the people around me, I also used the KASI House for our monthly board meetings. This is where, in fantastic surroundings, we could review the company's business plans, stroll down to the harbor and enjoy some Kobe beef, and then have a trance party on the boat until four in the morning. In the daytime, it was about making decisions and producing results; at night, partying, it was about opening up and forging the bonds that are so hugely important to get an international company to run like clockwork.

So, now, the question is whether the act of giving is something you can learn. For me, it has always felt completely natural. But not everyone can do it without a certain uneasiness, without feeling exploited, or without feeling that they are somehow losing themselves. That means we are really dealing with a quality that comes from the inside. And it is a quality that people will have to varying degrees. In a culture like the Danish one, we should note that the go-giver is navigating very narrow straits. Generally, our society is built on the idea that by paying our taxes we are helping the weak, and that by donating money to relief organizations we get to feel good about ourselves and take responsibility. To me, a go-giver is not a person who donates money to clear his or her conscience, but a person who simply *must* experience other people's happiness and enrichment to have a meaningful existence.

Thus, the KASI House represents a place designed to enrich the people around me, but also to create an inner state that would cause them to be willing to go the extra mile each day for their company and me. There have been situations where not even the KASI House was big enough and where I had to think along entirely new lines. One year, as our company was expanding at an extreme rate, I reached a point where my employees had run so fast, for so long, and worked so hard that I was having a difficult time looking them in the eye without feeling guilty. Everything I had done I had done in close partnership with my mom and my sister. Therefore, I sat down with them to mull over our next steps.

The year before, I had taken our entire staff to Bangkok to have a look at our production facilities over there. It was a business trip, but it also developed into an extraordinary vacation with lots of partying and fun. However, put gently, Bangkok does not exactly have a reputation for being a destination for people dedicated to upholding core family values. This created some tension among my employees' families, and so we had to refashion our approach. In consultation with my family, I decided that this time I would book a large luxury resort in southern Europe for a long weekend stay. To get there, I rented an Airbus A330 and loaded up with employees, sweethearts, spouses, and their kids. On the trip, I made sure they were given every imaginable service, treat, and delicacy. The whole shebang cost around

$700,000, but since, in the time leading up to the plane ride, we had sales of more than $140 million, with a very high contribution margin, this was a drop in the bucket. On the trip there were kids everywhere—and bringing the kids produced a fantastic openness. People played beach volleyball, basketball, soccer, held parties, went hiking. It created a unique energy and closeness and forged some completely fresh bonds crisscrossing our organization—priceless in both human and business terms. People were elated and could not wait to return to work to put in an even bigger effort. You can get part of the way to success by paying people a good wage; but you can go a great deal further if you are willing to enrich them with some unforgettable experiences.

Several years later, the Danish tax authorities had some issues regarding that particular trip. Under the tax rules, I was apparently not permitted to let the company pay for my employees' families. The authorities wanted to tax each individual employee for the trip. I refused and told them to send me the bill instead. I have regularly found myself in those kinds of situations, because I tend to do things that I feel are absolutely necessary. I could have been a stickler for the rules. I could have been better informed and realized from the outset that those kinds of things could not be done. This might have done wonders for my relationship with the authorities, but it would have made it really hard to create results on the scale that we did.

Stunt No. 2

Trust

On trusting in the best in people until proven wrong

As everyone who knows me is aware, I am unable to just sit still and watch television or hang about for any amount of time. I need to be active constantly. At one point, for example, I owned Germany's second-largest team handball club while also working on creating a new team handball club in my native country, Denmark. That same year when these two projects went into full bloom, my company, KASI Group, grew by upwards of $140 million. With the life I lead and the business my work generates, I have had to create a set of rules for how people can get in touch with me. For instance, if I let my employees and customers reach me by phone, I would be on the phone around the clock. Therefore, today, the only people I talk to on the phone are my closest relatives. My children, my sister, and my mom can always call me—but apart from them, I do not want to talk on the phone. To function in any kind of partnership with me, you will quickly realize that you cannot just call and get help if there are problems—you need to handle them yourself. I find it almost impossible to work with people whose first instinct is to reach for the phone or start typing a text message every time they encounter an obstacle. The fact that people need to call each other constantly to arrange meetings, when they are delayed, lost, or for thousands of other reasons is only an expression of a growing dependency on others. And that is something I really take issue with. For example, if we have arranged a meeting, sometimes people will ask me what to do if they are stuck in traffic or their car breaks down. Since I made the decision long ago for people not to call me, I naturally do not have a problem with people being delayed or not showing up for meetings. In fact, with respect to appointments, I am usually pretty indifferent. And as long as I do not have back-to-back appointments, I have no problem waiting around. Mentally, I am the type who is seized by being in whatever place I am at the time, and I do not generally pay a great deal of attention to what I am doing afterward. Because that is the way I feel, I have often had to hire people who would take me to the appointments that were important for me to keep and prioritize my schedule. Because I have complete confidence and trust in others, I never get angry or make a scene if people are late. In my mind, no one is late on purpose, and I know that people will have done everything in their power to come on time. In other words, if it does happen, it is never their fault. The important thing to me in working with other people is never about whether they are good at keeping appointments or getting to meetings on time, but whether they are competent and whether they can deliver on the agreements we have.

So, I have my own approach to using phones, and this naturally also goes for e-mailing. Everyone working with me knows that I always answer relevant e-mails within 24 hours, but not if they are longer than ten lines. On the other hand, I am 100% present at meetings and will happily stay behind to explain things several times if that is what it takes. It sometimes seems that people have been culturally conditioned or indoctrinated to call each other constantly to discuss or update each other on the smallest problems. My particular approach requires me to match my lack of presence on the telephone with a corresponding ability to be present in a different way. To me, physical presence is absolutely critical in generating the energy required to make a partnership work—you might call this "energy trust."

Trust is a state that is created between people who have the courage to open up to each other. If there is genuine trust between people, it takes a lot for conflicts, gossip, and misunderstandings to take root. As far as I am concerned, my primary task when I put together a team for a project is to create trust. My desire to generate that trust is both my greatest weakness and my greatest strength and has created quite a lot of noise in my life over the years. I have always believed that people's intentions are inherently good and that they mean me well. This means that whenever I do run into people with hidden agendas, I am usually completely trapped. This view of human nature is something I am really glad I have in 99 percent of all cases—that is the worldview that has allowed me to create the results I have. By meeting another person in what might look like blind trust from the beginning, I create a certain energy. That person before me will, in almost all cases, have to reciprocate. After all, for most people, by far, it takes a lot to let down someone who has come to you in blind faith. If someone does disappoint you, you need some kind of valve that you can shut off; one that is both withdrawn and cynical. The saying goes: Trust is good but control is better. For me, the opposite has always been the case, and that is why I work with 100% trust. I never have had and never will have control over my employees or business partners. Naturally, this only applies up to a certain point. The moment I feel that the trust I show them is no longer reciprocated, I will turn on a dime and become tough as nails and unyielding. Once that happens, I do not harbor any pangs of regret—I close down, create distance, and get rid of them. But, in principle, that is never really how it is. When someone else and I start a new relationship, I have to believe that the person I meet wants only the best for me, himself, and everyone else. The quality I am describing here can be fantastic and generate options and opportunities you never knew existed.

If you want to create trust, there is nothing more important than honesty. Of course, in business you cannot always play with open cards and let everyone in on your plans. But having hidden agendas to deceive people, to me, is something quite different. At the start of my career, I would sometimes say one thing but mean something different; I soon realized that this behavior introduces too many layers of complexity. Today, I say what I think with almost no filter, regardless of the person I meet. The downside, of course, is that if you do not have that filter, you are left completely open and vulnerable to people who are cynical and dishonest. And, regretfully, I have had that experience a number of times. Whenever that has happened, it has been a result of a person going out of his way to trick me, and every time it has caused me great personal distress, pain, and disappointment. But once my pain is gone, I also let go of my disappointment and move on. By the same token, I have always been very willing to forgive, regardless of what happened.

To illustrate this, I had an employee back in 2007 who wanted a seat on my board of directors. The only problem was that he did not have the right profile—I was looking for someone who could contribute a specific human element and create an open mood. In fact, in business it is not that hard to find people who know how to do tons of technical stuff, create spreadsheets, or manage warehouses. Those kinds of people pour forth in the thousands each year from business schools and similar institutions. No, what I need on my board are not skilled technicians but people capable of moving other people at a personal level. Even as I made it clear to this employee many times over that he was not a good fit for the board, he still pressed on. Finally, I sat him down and gently told him that it would never happen; he would never gain entry into the hallowed halls, and he needed to give up that dream. I then reminded him that he already had an incredibly exciting job that made it possible for him to drive a Porsche and that I was paying him quite a high wage each month. When he left me that day he was angry and upset, and a couple of days later, he came into my office with an ultimatum: unless I made him executive director he would quit. Naturally, I refuse to give in to such kinds of ultimatums, so I let him know that—if he really insisted on a board seat—he would have no other option than to quit. He quit. But as it turned out, those were not his final words in that case. And had I known what he had up his sleeve, I would have taken a number of precautions which - in my naïveté – would never have occurred to me back then.

I guess, at one point, this person had helped me prepare a number of presentations which we had saved to my computer. I had given him access to my computer, and as he and I were winding up our business relationship, he started reading my correspondence with my business partners, employees, family, and customers. This continued even after he had left the company completely. He went to great lengths to conceal his deception, going through servers in Canada and elsewhere, which meant that it was virtually impossible for anyone to spot when he would log onto my e-mail account. Unfortunately for him, he slipped up, presumably out of laziness, and logged on from his personal computer a couple of times, and this eventually enabled the police to track him down and map out his various moves. Unfortunately for me, if you saw—with no context whatsoever supplied—how my partners and I communicate, you would be shocked at how straightforward and rough our language is. We are trying to pull together thousands of strands; it is a big business; tons of energy are expended, and sometimes—in the heat of battle--language suffers. There are e-mails that say: "Get it under control!", "What the hell is going on here? Those prices are not supposed to go up!", or in a contract negotiation, I might write: "If I don't get this or this, go screw yourselves!"

The disgruntled employee took my various e-mails and somehow also managed to gain access to other accounts. He compiled quite a lot of e-mail exchanges and then took them to the press. During that same period, I had become a key sponsor for an international soccer team, so this was like dangling raw meat before a pack of starving wolves: "Take a look at this: Look how this guy is talking to his suppliers! Who does he think he is? Whoa, is that how he talks to his bankers?" This made me front-page news fodder for quite a while, and a public image was painted of me that I could have done without. It took me years to unscramble that mess.

Many people would no doubt use that kind of experience as evidence that life is unfair or that people are out to get them. They might even see themselves as victims, naïve, and start suspecting everyone they meet. Of course, it is always unpleasant to be attacked, but it is really dangerous to start down the path where you take setbacks as an invitation to cultivate your own angst or paranoia. Some people use most of their lives putting up locks, cameras, and alarms around their properties; they spend fortunes on insurance policies, legal advice, and attorneys. As soon as you go that route, you are looking at a self-perpetuating and limiting destructive cycle. As you get caught up in expanding your control of others, scanning for ulterior motives and spending all your energy on studying how you can avoid being cheated, you also let go of your freedom, your ability to soar above it all and see the full picture. In spite of the various bad experiences I have had with people over the years— people who have tried to trick or cheat or defraud me—I have always been determined not to let it make me paranoid or scared. Distrusting the world or other people can become the organism that makes your business wither on the vine. That is why I have always—with my head held high—made sure to grin and bear it and then put it all behind me in order to move forward. My basic way of doing business is about creating a foundation that permits my employees to have maximum trust and freedom—this, in turn, will make them assume a good deal of responsibility with respect to the roles they play. If, based on a number of unfortunate experiences, I would start down the control path, my philosophy would quickly be eroded, and my time as a successful businessman would end very quickly. It is not until trust has completely failed that you have a need for control, and once you can let go of that control, it is about getting back to trusting people as quickly as possible.

Jesper Nielsen

Life Story

The way to Pandora

On growing up, passions and my entry into the jewelry industry

I am originally from a small suburb of the Danish capital, Copenhagen. My dad was an electrician and my mom was a homemaker for many years. My big sister, Annette, and I had a very harmonious childhood with parents who genuinely cared for us in all imaginable ways. During my childhood and school days, team handball and soccer were especially important to the family. My dad played handball at the elite level, and I learned how to count by looking at the scoreboard when I accompanied him to his training. I started out by playing soccer when I was five years old and handball when I was eight. With respect to school, I was bone lazy but somehow still managed to continue receiving top grades in almost all of my classes.

At school, there was only one thing—apart from soccer and handball—I felt truly passionate about. When I reached my teens, disk jockeys had gone from just flipping records to something special. The disk jockey was often the focal point of big parties and had a kind of license to put a creative touch on the music. The first time I experienced this phenomenon, I was completely sold. As a disk jockey, you are not only a performer but the person responsible for getting the party going, whipping people into a frenzy, moving people from mood to mood—just the right role for me. After my confirmation, I managed to barely scrape together enough cash to buy a sound mixer, which my dad and I hooked up to two turntables. With my headset, I would stand there all day in my room and play and mix music, eyes closed imagining the energy on the dance floor. Some of the bands—which now seem virtually antiquated and quaint—that absorbed me the most during this period were Duran Duran and Adam and the Ants. Then, there was Bob Marley, another favorite of mine. But one day my sister introduced me to Bruce Springsteen, and that was it for me! To me, Springsteen's sound was just completely authentic, and my clear favorite was his album "The River." I most liked the title track, which had everything—both in respect to music and lyrics. Over the years, I was completely captivated by Springsteen's unique ability to describe the simplicity in those small things that are wholly universal and critical no matter who you are, what you own, and what you are able to do. My parents were also fascinated by Springsteen's music, and we had some fantastic experiences whenever he would issue new albums or when we managed to get tickets to his concerts. In positive contrast to the relative tedium at school, all the music that preoccupied me became a universe where I found meaning and depth. Every cent I could get my hands on was spent on new records or to expand my sound mixer. My room ended up being jam-packed with records and equipment, and on the weekends I would earn a few bucks disk jockeying at local parties.

At school, my teachers were worried: To them, I did not seem to devote any special energy on anything worthwhile. Once primary school ended—in 10th grade in Denmark—I, along with around 24 boys and girls, enrolled in Denmark's first team handball secondary school program. The simplest way to describe team handball, or just "handball," to non-Europeans, is that it is what basketball is to Americans. It is a fast and incredibly physical game estimated to have nearly 800,000 teams playing throughout the world. In Europe, it is second only to soccer in popularity. We attended normal classes in the mornings and then did handball in the afternoons. In the Danish high school system, you can choose to focus on either languages or math and sciences. I chose languages, but not for any particularly profound reason. At that time in my life, I was all about just finding the shortest possible path to my goal. And since languages came fairly easily to me, it was not a particularly hard choice. I finished high school with average grades. In fact, I had been under a good deal of stress at times because I had been absent so many days, and because I quite simply did not do my homework. I was regularly called in for interviews with my teachers who were always wondering why I was not living up to my potential. The only problem was that the potential they saw was not the potential I wanted to cultivate, and the potential I wanted to cultivate was not one that was being supported in high school.

After high school, I continued on to business school more or less on autopilot. But after three short months I realized that there was no use in continuing. It quickly became quite clear to me that what I was learning there was never going to be anything I would have any use for. Most of the stuff was far too theoretical for me, with little obvious practical value. However, back in high school I had started working at the local gas station mart. It was in this job, to a much greater degree, that I really felt I was learning things directly applicable to my life that might benefit me for the rest of my life. To me, school represented what was academic and pretentious, whereas the gas station mart represented freedom and what was genuine. In this after-school job, I learned about purchase prices, sale prices, procurement, disposition, and invoicing. My day-to-day manager at the mart must have thought he had struck pure gold having me on the staff. My approach to the job was completely uncompromising: I wanted to soak up everything—and everything he proposed was feasible. This meant that he could call me 15 minutes before a shift started to let me know someone had called in sick; before he had time to finish his sentence, I was on the road. That job attitude was something that was really appreciated, and gradually I was put on more and more shifts. After I had worked there for a while, I started coming in early to open the gas station at 6:00 in the morning, leaving again at 7:50 a.m. This allowed me to get to high school just in the nick of time. A little too often I would take the entire day off from high school—I just preferred being at work.

It is probably no surprise that I quite quickly developed a great relationship with my boss. But I also had fantastic relationships with my customers; in fact, I even managed to become a kind of gathering point for the entire area as all my friends would come in for a quick chat. At one point, a competing gas station chain made me a very tempting offer. I told my boss, and he told me it would be a shame if the gas station chain would lose me to one of their competitors. He quickly asked me if he could recommend me as "second-in-command" at a new 24-hour gas station mart for the same company I was already working for. The new gas station mart was the biggest in Denmark, located right off a major highway exit outside Copenhagen. I was pretty excited about this, and soon I was busy working at what was the ultimate job to me at the time. My new boss at the 24-hour mart was not only an incredibly nice and sympathetic guy but also insanely competent. Working under him I learned every little detail of running a major retail outlet. He immediately delegated a lot responsibility to me. For example, one weekend *he* would manage the gas station; the next weekend *I* managed everything. Whenever there were evening or night shifts where we could not find any staff, I stepped up to the plate. What could be a better training ground? As an employee, I was firing on all cylinders, and my attitude to things meant that my boss always knew that someone had his back and that the business was in good hands when I was on duty.

I worked at that 24-hour mart for more than two years before my boss decided to move on. But before he did so, he asked what I thought about perhaps getting my own gas station mart. It had of course crossed my mind before, and I thought it sounded very exciting. I was put in touch with a gas station chain that was looking for franchisees. As a franchisee, I would simply take over a gas station with staff and everything. I would then purchase the goods from the company, sell them to the customers, and keep the profits. To get started, I called the regional manager for the gas station mart chain. He was absolutely perplexed that a kid like me, aged 24 years, wanted to run a gas station by himself. After going over my background, he was convinced that I could manage it, and soon I became the youngest franchisee in the company's history. Now I had my own gas station, which was near a heavily trafficked feeder road to a major urban area. Each morning I would open the gas station at 6:30 a.m. and work hard into the very late hours. It was often pretty hard work, but I felt that everything I did during the day was exceptionally instructive and exciting. After a year at the gas station, the regional boss was pretty impressed. He saw how I had managed to get a gas station that was already doing fine to increase sales by almost 30 percent. Apart from this, he could not help noticing that the gas station was shining like a mirror. He remarked that I seemed to have an unnatural abundance of energy and asked me how I might feel about running two gas stations. And, sure enough, soon after that I had a second gas station in the area. Six months later, yet another gas station became available, and the regional manager told me that there was no reason to go out and look for a new person to take it over if I was interested. Instead, I could have that gas station for the asking.

Before I reached the age of 25, I was the only person who had ever franchised three gas station marts at the same time in Denmark. The businesses went swimmingly, everything was working out great, and it felt quite natural to me to run a business that was open 365 days a year, from 6:00 in the morning until midnight every evening with 40 employees and annual sales slightly shy of $30 million. Managing something of that magnitude became a kind of elementary school for me as a manager, and there is no doubt that it helped shape my approach to work later on in life. After nearly five years with my gas stations, it was still going well. And even as I earned a lot of money, I was nonetheless thinking about whether this was what I wanted to spend the rest of my life on. Frankly, I felt I had too much energy to continue this way until I was 50. I started looking around for something else. One day I saw a job ad in a newspaper for a regional manager for a nationwide supermarket chain. If I could get that job, I would no longer just be in charge of three stores but 20 stores. I sent them an application and got the job.

In the beginning, my dad and I tried to partner up so that he could continue the gas stations, but the chain would not agree to that. The gas stations had to be wound down, and while that was going on, something happened that turned my life upside-down. From my accounts, the accountants could see that I had leased some car washing facilities and depreciated them as if they had been purchased. This was an error, and once that was corrected, my profits had turned into a loss. In order to be able to pay off this debt, I needed to sell everything I owned, and I still ended up with a whack to the head. Even as I had earned a lot of money, my private consumption was high—I lived expensively and had a couple of expensive cars. Once the accounts were drawn up, I still had about $135,000 outstanding debt. Frankly, that was a bit of a cold shower, but it was also the final lesson from my time as a self-employed worker. The lesson I learned was that I, in the future, needed to keep a much greater margin between my income and expenses. But I also learned how truly unpleasant it was to suddenly have all your credit cards seized and be declared personally bankrupt. If I had known things would turn out that way, I would naturally have kept my three gas stations and worked off the debt. But when the error was discovered, it was too late to turn back. This meant that—in spite of my high salary in my new job—I still had to pay monthly installments which meant that I could look forward, for the next many years, to live at the financial level of a welfare recipient. It is said that behind every successful businessman there is a bankruptcy or two—there is probably something to that. Among other things, my bankruptcy taught me how little money actually meant to me. Even though my lifestyle and circumstances had completely changed now, I was perfectly fine going forward. And since nothing I had done was about becoming wealthy, I also did not feel like a big dream of mine had been crushed. Throughout the bankruptcy, I realized that my business drive was not fueled by greed or a desire to achieve extreme affluence. What was important to me was growing a business and to see the people who are part of it develop and experience joy. Whether or not I was being paid, that was not the deciding factor. Money and financial gain was, in reality, only an indicator that I was using myself correctly and did what made sense to me.

During the following period, I was divorced from my wife and according to our agreement, we would see our kids on alternate weeks. At the same time, I worked for the supermarket and paid off a big part of my debt without anyone else, apart from me and my closest relatives, knowing anything about the bankruptcy. My new job was exceptionally exciting, and it taught me a lot about getting 20 store managers to succeed in 20 different stores, based on as many different business models. One of the reasons it went so well was that my boss quite quickly let me be Jesper Nielsen. To him, I seemed like an extraordinary breath of fresh air, and because of him, I was permitted to do things in my own special way. The stores I was dealing with were all situated in areas of Copenhagen inhabited by some of the bottom members of the social strata. This taught me what is required when you recruit employees who do not have the same secure upbringing I did. Daily, I was confronted by the dark side of life and witnessed what it meant to live a daily existence of problems like drinking, betrayal, violence, neglect, and many other tough conditions. In the stores, this often translated into problems with employees or problems with theft. Everyone's backgrounds and lots in life were different, and as the manager of the various stores, I needed to take all those into account. In several of the stores I worked with, there were quite a lot of immigrants from third-world countries. And to achieve success with them, I needed to do things completely differently than I was used to from my gas stations. It was a fantastic experience learning to work with so much diversity, because it showed me how important it is for a manager to put his own needs on hold and to be met in a certain way. If I was going to motivate and inspire this many people, with so many different backgrounds and qualifications, religious persuasions, and goals, I needed to tune into each individual and treat them differently from everyone else. My relationships with some of my employees back then later resulted in my taking them with me into my jewelry business where they were given elevated positions.

After having worked for four years for the supermarket chain, I was still incredibly happy with my job. At some point, however, I was given a new manager, and I quickly realized that my days in the chain in question were numbered. My new boss was the old-fashioned type who was managing according to a narrow set of principles and rules and who, in my eyes, would have been a better fit for the military. Here was a man who spent an inordinate amount of energy on showing how powerful he was and how dangerous it would be if you did not toe the line under his command.

Encountering him, I came to the realization that I really despised authority and having to work with people who are trying to control others but who have nothing special to offer at the purely professional level. To some people "control" becomes an all-consuming obsession, and this manager defined and limited himself in those terms. I started looking for something else to do. I particularly remember New Year's Eve 2001. My parents were looking after my two kids while I went shopping for groceries. There were still many years to come until I could pay my final debt installment from my bankruptcy, and I only had some spare change in my pockets—without a credit card there would be no extravagant New Year's party for the kids. That day it struck me that I needed to find a way to money—a way that would create more freedom for both me and my kids. I was not driven by money, but the thought of financial independence became more and more attractive to me. And if I were to experience this fully, that could only happen if I were completely independent.

During that same period, I had a friend who was selling jewelry in Norway. He would go there for trade shows, and I sometimes acted as his chauffeur: I paid for the drive, he paid for the booze, and that way we had some great trips together. My friend was not a great businessman, as he would probably be the first person to tell you, but I noticed on our trips that he nevertheless managed to sell some of his jewelry. I gradually started taking a greater interest in how things worked. And when I started understanding his relationships with his customers better, I asked him if I might have a go at selling some of his jewelry—in Germany. He gladly accepted. I took a 14-day vacation from my job at the supermarket and laid out a course for Germany with some jewelry boxes in the backseat. I had suggested Germany for no other immediate reason that I had been longing to go abroad. It did not hurt that it also happens to be a massive market with lots of money sloshing about. At the same time, I had long felt that there was something exciting waiting for me there.

On my trip, I stopped in Hamburg to start my sales tour. It soon became clear that my 14 days in Germany would be a bit of a challenge. I remember saying to myself: "Okay, you are driving down to a foreign country; you don't speak the language; you're not familiar with the culture. You will be selling a product there which you know nothing about to customers you have never met, and you have no idea how to find them." Still, I pulled my car into what seemed to me the best street in Hamburg, settled on the first jewelry store I saw, and cheerfully walked through the door with a box of jewelry under my arm. I went up to the counter, and started talking in my—very—broken German, gesticulating wildly. The poor man behind the counter must have thought I was completely insane. He did not buy anything, but that was perfectly okay with me. During our "conversation," I started getting ideas about how I might do better in the next place. Fourteen days later I drove back across the border to Denmark. I had managed to sell a grand total of three packages of jewelry, and my conclusion was crystal clear: If I could sell three packages, I could sell 300. And if I could sell 300, I could sell 1,000. When I got home, I pulled out my big map of Germany and started counting how many places I could sell jewelry. I still remember the sensation I had as I sat there planning my next trip: There was only one person who could halt the momentum and I was that person. It was with that gut feeling that I returned to work—to hand in my resignation.

I have never been the kind of person just to leave a company in a bad situation. I told my hyper-authoritative boss at the supermarket that my resignation did not have to be effective immediately. I was convinced that he would soon find a replacement for me, and once the new regional manager was in place I would ship out. My manager—or as he seemed to see himself, my commanding officer—was naturally shocked at my decision. It was beyond his realm of perception that anyone could be that reckless as not to have anything more definitive lined up before handing in his resignation. I am pretty sure he thought I had completely lost my grip on reality. If I thought I could just bumble around Germany at random and make a living from selling jewelry, I would have to be out of my mind. Two months later he had not found a replacement for me. I asked him what was going on, and he answered that he thought I had regretted my resignation. I let him know, in no uncertain terms, that I had not regretted it, and that he should hurry up and find a replacement so that I could return to Germany and continue my project. Nearly ten months went by before I finally managed to leave, and it was not until I finally set a definitive end date at which I would no longer come to work that he understood how serious I was.

The first thing that happened when I finally left the super-market chain was that I was classified a welfare recipient. The most immediate, beneficial effect this had on my cir-cumstances was that I no longer had to make payments on the debt from my personal bankruptcy. It also meant that the structure of my life improved quite a bit: I would drive around in Germany for one week, and on alternate weeks, I could be at home with my two kids. My kids were at just the right age for this, and because I was home when they were with me, their experience was that I was always at home. At the same time, I could let go of them every other week when they were staying with my ex-wife, and I was able to give it my all when I was in Germany. During the following months, through a lot of hard work, I found 60 customers in Germany and was now so sure of the potential that it was time to move into a higher gear. I transferred the 60 cus-tomers to my friend who was the dealer for the jewelry. The process had been incredibly instructive, and to me it was not important to earn money on this initial piece of work. My efforts had given me so much new knowledge about the potential for jewelry sales in Germany that I was certain that the time I had spent doing research there had been time incredibly well spent. I was now ready to start up for real. Soon after that, I entered into an agreement with an Italian jewelry firm to sell a jewelry collection called Vero Firenze in Germany. Vero Firenze was a steel bracelet based on a concept from the 1950s. The concept was that you would buy various items, which would allow you to design or put together your own piece of jewelry. For example, if you had been to Brazil, you could buy a Brazilian flag in gold or enamel. Let us say you had received a heart from your sweetheart or you wanted to show people that you were born in a specific sign of the Zodiac—with this bracelet, you could attach that heart, flag, or sign to the bracelet. This gives the bracelet a very personal touch which means that, by just looking at it, you can tell a lot of things about the person wearing it. In other words, the bracelet was not just a bracelet with a story, but also a reflection of the owner's personality, life, and experiences. The bracelet in question had been a huge international success since the mid-90s; the fact that the concept was well-established and familiar in the market made it easier for me to approach customers than if I had started out by selling something completely new and unknown.

After signing the agreement with Vero Firenze, I met with my sister and my parents to see if they wanted to help me. I needed some start-up capital and I needed help. My family was immediately interested. There was no doubt that my family could feel that I had both a vision and an abundance of energy. My parents took out a loan on their house so we could get started. We then jointly decided who was going to do what. My dad would be the person packing up the jewelry, making sure packages would get off to the post office. My mom would do the invoicing once she got home from her job at the Danish national lottery, and my sister stepped in with legal expertise when she came home from her job as a lawyer at the Danish Ministry of Foreign Affairs. I became a consultant to the company who, once a week, was sent to Germany in the cheapest possible rental car we could find or in my dad's old battered Opel. We also established a company, and since I was still declared bankrupt, we initially had to incorporate it under my mom's name. On my first sales tour, after selling the first jewelry package, it suddenly occurred to me that we still had not named our business. I therefore called my mom back in Denmark to ask her to put on her thinking cap and figure something out. She turned it over in her head for a couple of hours; she tried to combine family members' names in creative ways but could not come up with anything that sounded exactly right. In the end, she asked herself what exactly I was out there doing. Based on the initial letters for the Danish word she believed covered our business enterprise, she formed the acronym "KASI." At first, I thought that sounded pretty peculiar for a company name. But my mom had made up her mind, so I decided not to give it much more thought. And that was how the KASI Group was officially incorporated in Denmark in 2003. At about the same time, we established our first office in an industrial business park and furnished it with an old dining table purchased at a flea market, along with another dining table made available by my parents. This meant that my parents had no dining table for many months.

All the world's successful brands—regardless of whether they are Gucci, Bestseller, or H&M—were started by someone who was unusually good at selling stuff. You can produce the perfect product. But if there is no one to create and structure a distribution network and execute sales, that product will go absolutely nowhere. I am not just talking about pushing items across a counter but about being able to create a universe with the capacity to *really* engage customers. Apart from that, you also need a bit of luck meeting the right people; you need to enter the market with the right product at the right time; and you need to be cheeky and creative enough to make use of the opportunities you see at precisely the moment they arise. In my work, I was naturally extraordinarily hard-working and spent an enormous amount of hours on my venture. This meant that I gradually became familiar with all the German hamlets, towns, and cities. I was like a fish in water moving around Germany. This naturally has numerous drawbacks and costs with respect to other facets of life, but if you want to succeed, you need to be ready to bet everything you have.

Many have later asked me how I managed to have the impact I did in Germany. The fact is that I was bold enough to believe that it could be done, but it was also invaluable that I was able to think like a German—be like a German—was able to breathe in the German culture and be part of the energy that that country has to offer. If you want to be successful in a country, it is not enough just to visit. You need to live there and be able to feel you are a part of what goes on there. There are an enormous number of businesses from small countries that try to start up in big countries, and they are often surprised at how difficult it is. If a country is ten times as big as your own country, it is not ten times as easy to break into—on the contrary. In large countries, all the major players are on the pitch at the same time; and this means that competition is far tougher than in small countries. An effort with just a few sales reps might be all right for a country with just a few million inhabitants, but in a large country, a small-scale effort might very well be drowned out in the noise. This meant that my tiny one-man enterprise in a wretched little car with overnight stays at dodgy hotels at the outskirts of cities just did not cut it. So, it was a bit of a coincidence when something happened that turned the KASI Group's activities upside-down in Germany. In my work with the Vero Firenze jewelry, I would always make sure I left my brochures everywhere I went. One day I received a call from an elderly gentleman who had seen one of my brochures. He wanted to know if he could sell Vero Firenze for me. First, I did not quite catch his drift. I asked him if he meant *buying* jewelry from me.

"No, no," he said. "I want to bring your jewelry along with me when I am out in the stores anyway, and then get a commission on what I sell."

"Sure, yes, absolutely!" I exclaimed. I was completely taken aback and thought how nice it would be if I was not the only person selling Vero Firenze in the German market.

"But, listen, how much of a commission did you have in mind?"

"Oh, 15 to 20 percent," he said.

Since my own profit was around 60 percent, this sounded quite reasonable. If I gave him 20 percent, there was still 40 percent left over for me. When I took the call, I was on my way back to Denmark from southern Germany, and I had had customer meetings all day long. I suggested that we could meet at a rest stop farther north toward Denmark around midnight.

"Midnight?" he cried out. He might have thought it was a strange time to meet, but nevertheless, he showed up. After an hour-long discussion, I gave him a package of jewelry, 100 product catalogs, and a form with instructions for how to sign up new customers. A week later, he had brought in five new customers, and I very quickly realized that that form of partnership gave my business a completely new dimension. I asked the man if he happened to have some friends who might also want to deal Vero Firenze jewelry. It turned out that he had a whole network of friends all over Germany who wanted in. After that episode, I started devoting a much greater share of my time going to Germany to find people who could find new customers for me.

In 2004, KASI Group really started picking up speed. To be able to keep up with the increasing sales and work pressure, my mom resigned from her job at the Danish national lottery and transitioned into working full-time for the KASI Group. My sister and dad also had their hands full. Before the end of my first year with Vero Firenze, we had such a tailwind that I managed to establish about 20 independent German sales representatives who drove around Germany selling jewelry for the KASI Group. Naturally, not all the sales reps I found performed equally well. Some disappeared with the jewelry, others did nothing at all, but most, by far, worked very efficiently and gradually grew our customer base to a level that made our activities in Germany a pretty lucrative business. One thing I learned during that time of my life was not to spend time looking back. If we had acquired 100 customers, there might be 40 who did not quite work out, but instead of focusing on the ones that did not work out, it was all about moving on and on creating new customers. We constantly pressed on: Every time we made a mistake or signed a contract with someone who did not perform as expected, we picked up whatever experience we could and continued full steam ahead to create our next customer. Every day during this period, I was focused on only three things, 24 hours a day—distribution, distribution, and more distribution.

The start of the business adventure

Meeting with Pandora

*On accomplishing the impossible and making the impossible
a habit*

The first time I encountered Pandora jewelry was at a jewelry trade show in Denmark in 2004. Since I had started selling Vero Firenze in 2003, I had managed to build a network
of around 1,500 customers and a very effective sales structure in Germany where we had jewelry sales of slightly less
than $11 million that first year. Even though my family and
I were doing really well and making a good living from our
collaboration with Vero Firenze, I was still looking around
for other areas to cultivate or trying to find something that
might supplement my collection.

At the trade show in Denmark, I checked out various collections and was not entirely sure what to choose. All I
knew was that I really wanted to supplement my collection
with another type of assembled jewelry—even though many
people had told me that that the "collector's mania" would
probably end soon. I was pretty sure it would not. Those
who were skeptical back then with respect to assembled
jewelry generally thought the collector's mania was a new
phenomenon, and that—as with so many other trends—it
would quickly run its course. Assembled jewelry, however,
is not a fresh invention; this kind of jewelry has existed in
various guises pretty much since the Viking Age when the
first explorers were poking around for something to give to

their wives back home. And it is pretty clear that women throughout history have not become any less interested in collecting—quite the opposite.

One of the collections I looked at when I arrived at the fair was by the producer of a brand called Lovelinks. I also looked at Troldbeads and Unodomani and then, of course, also at Pandora. I walked around the exhibition hall where there were four different collections that all looked promising, each in their own way. As I was talking to the various wholesalers' representatives, it became more and more difficult for me to decide which way to go. At that time, I was still relatively new in the business, and frankly, I had a difficult time telling one product from the next. If you asked the manufacturers, you would get the same exactly predictable story how *their* product was the best. But when I asked why that particular product was the best, none of them could convince me why I should choose one over another. Once a trend picks up momentum, a great number of different brands will pop up that look pretty similar. Every trend has a self-reinforcing effect, and the more money there is in the trend in question, the more difficult it is to tell one brand from the next. For that reason, it is easy to spend an inordinate amount of time discussing raw materials, stones, designs, surface treatment, or talking about the various ways they will appeal to customers. In reality, none of these qualities are essential to making a collection strong. The most important features are how the items are marketed, how they are distributed, and whether you have the wherewithal to brand the product properly. As far as my difficult choice at the trade show was concerned, my final decision was eventually based on a bit of a coincidence. As I was strolling about looking at the various pieces of jewelry, I happened to run into Kenneth Ramstrup, one of the founders of Pandora. We immediately had good chemistry, but we also discovered that we were fans of the Danish soccer club, Brøndby IF. Of course, this meant I had to go with Pandora.

Pandora's position today is that they—and they alone—dominate the world market within assemblage jewelry. And this is in spite of around a hundred registered so-called look-alikes that operate on the basis of a somewhat similar concept. For regular people, it may be difficult to understand how Pandora could grow to that size. In actuality, it is a very simple concept that consists of a snake bracelet. For the bracelet, you can use beads or, as with Vero Firenze, you can collect or design your own piece of jewelry.

The first time I saw Pandora's products at the trade show, no one outside of people in Denmark knew anything about them. The firm was started by Per Enevoldsen who had run a small jeweler's shop in Copenhagen since 1982. At some point he had started going to Thailand where he had some jewelry manufactured that he brought home to sell from his store. In this way, over time, he had created a small jewelry distribution company and had allied himself with a very proactive and capable salesman by the name of Kenneth Ramstrup. For Kenneth, his partnership had been vaguely frustrating: He was driving around Denmark trying to sell jewelry for the company, which was then called Populær A/S. Put plainly, these were seriously boring pieces made of nice silver. In order to get their business going, Populær attempted to undercut their competitors and then continue to purchase items in India which would then be sold as cheaply as possible. Populær's jewelry had no story—no brand or anything else that might make it interesting to customers.

When Kenneth visited jewelers or goldsmiths they would often show him the jewelry from Vero Firenze, telling him how smart that concept was. Kenneth was not particularly impressed by the craftsmanship of Vero Firenze, and he became more and more irritated that customers would even buy that kind of thing. In the end, he contacted Per Enevoldsen and asked him if he could produce a piece of jewelry based on the same idea, but use proper and professional craftsmanship. In other words, Kenneth wanted to keep the concept and just change the product. Thus, the two of them started what was to become the foundation of the first Pandora jewelry. The pioneering work they did took place in 1998 and 1999, and in 2000 they were ready to put Pandora on the market. It is important to bear in mind that this was not at all the Pandora that later spread like wildfire across the globe. For example, in the beginning they used oxidized silver, which was a little too dark for my taste. It was only much later that it developed into the colorful and more varied Pandora jewelry we see today.

Nevertheless, Kenneth managed to sell a starting package with jewelry to a jeweler back in 2000. And with smarts and hard work, Kenneth managed to get Pandora off the ground in Denmark. When I met Kenneth at the jewelry fair in 2004, Pandora had already become a fad in Denmark. But, as I noted before, no one was familiar with the brand in other countries. There were a couple of distributors in Belgium and Norway who were browsing, but they were not yet serious.

The fact that the name of the jewelry collection became Pandora is something that people have been wondering about since it began. Pandora, of course, is a Greek goddess—and most people have heard about Pandora's Box, which contained all the evils in the world. From a marketing perspective, this is not a particularly helpful story. The reason Per and Kenneth chose the name Pandora has to do with the fact that they, as they were developing the concept, had hired a small ad agency to come up with various suggestions to how the new jewelry might be presented and what its name should be. At that time, they had a messenger girl at Populær who also did the cleaning and helped doing small chores around the office. When she heard that they were in the process of finding a name for their new jewelry collection, she said that her mother had said that she thought that the name Pandora was ideal for a jewelry collection. Once the ad men heard that, it just resonated with them. They looked it up and started investigating what it might sound like pronounced in various languages and were gradually completely convinced that Pandora should be the name for the new collection.

As mentioned, most have heard of Pandora's Box as part of Greek mythology. There are many versions of this story, but according to the one most people know, one of the Greek gods had a weakness for mortals. He therefore gave human beings fire so that they could be warm, find their way at night, and prepare food. The other gods were afraid that humans would use fire for evil, and upon Zeus's order,

Pandora was made from water and earth for the purpose of punishing humans. All the Greek gods gave Pandora gifts—among other things, Beauty, Charm, Intelligence, and Curiosity. The last gift, from Zeus, was a box. She was told never to open it. But since Pandora had also been given the gift of Curiosity, she could not stop thinking about what might be inside the box. In the end, it was too much for Pandora who could no longer resist the temptation. She lifted the lid to cast a quick glance at the secrets inside the box. But when the lid was opened, all the human evils escaped from the box: from Greed to Vanity, Gossip, Envy, and many other mortal sins. A terrified Pandora slammed the lid back on. In doing so, she preserved what was left in the box, which were all the beautiful things—Love, Hope, Passion, and other qualities humans were thus allowed to keep.

When the people at the jewelry firm, Pandora, are talking about Pandora's Box, they are referring to the customer opening up the box to let something out. But what are left in are all the beautiful things Pandora is famous for making. During the years I worked with Pandora, we turned and twisted that story around multiple times—anyone with the slightest knowledge of marketing told us that Pandora was an unusually poor name to sell a product. However, what is interesting is that many people are currently more familiar with the jewelry from Pandora than with the mythology behind the story about Pandora's Box.

At the trade show, Kenneth was happy when I told him that I was interested in dealing Pandora in Germany. Denmark is a tiny country, and the German market is nearly 15 times bigger than the Danish one. In his eagerness to get to Germany, Kenneth immediately started talking about a cooperation agreement. However, I preferred that we take a slightly more informal approach and suggested instead that we—before drawing up a formal agreement—take a small, improvised trip to Germany. This would give us a chance to get to know each other while also giving him some idea about what exactly I could do in my newly acquired market. Based on that, I purchased ten starting packages from Pandora, and arranged to meet Kenneth at one of the big German rest areas. From there, the plan was that we would drive out to some German jewelry stores and show them the jewelry. This would let us assess if there was any interest in Germany and allow Kenneth to have a look at the various jewelry stores and determine who he wanted as Pandora's customers in Germany.

Some three weeks later I received the jewelry, and I showed them to some German jewelry people. They all just shrugged and told me that they did not think the jewelry pieces were particularly exciting. According to them, they looked too Indian and hippie-like—but of course everyone is a bit skeptical the first time they see something new. I thought the feedback I had received from the Danish market was good, and I had a strong gut feeling about the items. Luckily, I chose to trust that instinct.

Everyone who knows me knows that I am a pretty straightforward businessman: I say what is on my mind and stand by what I say. At the same time, I have also been quoted as saying that a good salesman succeeds through fabrication but is remembered for his honesty. If you want to go far as a salesman, you need to firmly believe in your products, naturally, but if you lack the boldness to be just a little cheeky or take chances once in a while, it is pretty safe to say that you will never be successful in that profession. I charted out a ballsy strategy with respect to Kenneth who, of course, was a salesman himself. I needed to convince him that I was the best salesman he had ever met, thus paving the way for a contract with Pandora that was as advantageous to me as possible. So, when we met at the rest stop, we set out for Hanover in northern Germany which was the next big city along the highway. Kenneth, cautious as ever, asked me if I thought I might perhaps need a GPS device. I told him no and explained to him that Germany was my second home and that I knew pretty much all the roads across the entire country. With a suitably impressed Kenneth in the passenger's seat, we soon made it to Hanover and parked outside one of Germany's truly large jewelry stores.

Naturally, I did not exactly need clairvoyant skills to be able to predict that this was a store Kenneth would be ecstatic to have as a customer for Pandora. However, what Kenneth did not know was that I was in the process of executing my strategy. I knew that Kenneth spoke next to no German and that he would not be able to understand anything if I just talked fast enough. I had also called the owner of the store ahead of the visit telling him that I would arrive that same day with a Dane who understood very little German. Together with the Dane, I would present a new product which the jeweler would enthusiastically accept. The jeweler also promised me that he would tell my Danish companion that this was exactly the kind of product he had been waiting for. Before I hung up, I promised the jeweler that he did not need to pay for the jewelry upon delivery. He could naturally return the jewelry free of charge at any time. The jeweler had no problems with that arrangement, and when Kenneth and I entered the shop, we were welcomed with open arms. As usual, I showed up without a jacket and tie, and for a full hour, I talked (in my rapid-fire, near grammar-free German) about soccer with the store's owner. Kenneth tried to follow the conversation, but even if he was pretty much just a bystander he was nevertheless impressed that my customer contact was *that* informal. Once we had had our fill of soccer chit-chat, we moved on to the items Kenneth and I were there to show him. And that was how Pandora's jewelry was put on a German counter for the first time. With the jewelry before him, the jeweler straightened up and expressed the kind of excitement we had arranged beforehand. I was afraid he might have overdone it when he left us to fetch the rest of his staff. Soon, we were surrounded by a crowd for what seemed an eternity admiring Kenneth's jewelry. In the meantime I was looking at Kenneth asking him if this was the kind of customers he wanted. Obviously, Kenneth's eyes were wide with wonder and opportunity, and after having sold a package to the enthusiastic jeweler, we got back into my car and continued to a jewelry store in the next major city.

In the next city, the owner of the store—the biggest jewelry store in the city—was a woman. She had also been prepped for our visit and was perfectly willing to buy Pandora's jewelry without having even seen it. With her, I was not discussing soccer but fashion, and in that area I had also developed a certain knowledge that could create the completely informal mood we needed before I played my trump card by showing her Kenneth's jewelry. With great enthusiasm she, too, ordered a package before an overawed Kenneth Ramstrup. We continued on to the next city where we also sold a package, and when the day came to an end, an impressed Kenneth asked how many customers I thought I might be able to find in Germany.

I already had some 1,500 potential customers in my network, but since we had just sold to three of them, I told him that there was no reason why the remaining 1,497 would not also buy his jewelry. Deliveries of that magnitude were far more than Kenneth could handle. He had production facilities he needed to consider, and he proposed that, for the first year, I would have to be content with selling to 35 select customers. I accepted and with the contract in hand, I had paved the way to sell Pandora jewelry—even if I still did not have any actual proof that the jewelry would sell.

One of my greatest challenges was that I did not think Pandora catered to quite the same stores as Vero Firenze. Vero Firenze was not the same quality as Pandora, and Pandora needed to be sold by the top jewelers in the various metropolitan centers. My first step in the process was not so much about the jewelers but about convincing my German sales representatives that they should now also sell for Pandora. At the same time, it was not enough that they just sold the product. They needed to feel in their bones that this was the exactly right product at exactly the right time. If I could not rally them around Pandora and get them really excited, our fire would quickly be extinguished. Naturally, folders, displays, brochures, and all other kinds of materials needed to be produced, but all those details I quickly got out of the way. And then it was time to talk to the sales representatives.

The reception of Pandora's jewelry among my German sales representative was, as I had expected, mixed. About half were convinced that they would never *ever* be able to sell Pandora in the stores. Usually when I have a vision, I easily get so excited that I will run almost to the goal line long before others sense that that they could or should cross the midfield. In my meetings with the sales representatives, I made sure to hold back and not put my proverbial horse before the cart. If I revealed too much, those who were skeptical might easily think I had lost contact with reality. I spent quite a good deal of time listening to the skeptics and their concerns. When I started out with Vero Firenze, I had personally visited many stores and seen in person how difficult it can be to break through in the stores. So I had some credibility when I told the sales reps that I understood how they felt about presenting something completely new. To see something you have never seen before means that you get in touch with the core of who you are as a human being. Some react by lifting their arms over their heads and diving right in. But those are not necessarily the ones who will be able to create the best results. To me, a positive situation arises when people see something new and are able to relate critically to it. When we started with Vero Firenze, it was something that some people were familiar with. But Pandora was completely unknown, and it was only natural that the sales reps would greet the collection with a healthy dose of skepticism. We decided that we would build up our interaction with stores gradually and organically until they started trusting our product. We made the first Pandora starting packages quite small; and as sales representatives soon reported back from the field that the packages were starting to move, more and more sales reps came on board.

Already a few weeks after my trip with Kenneth, I had around 200 customers ready to sell Pandora's products with many more waiting in the wings. All the orders were transmitted on to Pandora with lightning speed, and they fought a valiant battle to keep up with demand. Soon, I was phoned by a slightly out-of-breath Kenneth who could not quite comprehend how 35 customers could reorder at such a breathless pace. He asked me if I was absolutely sure we were only selling to 35 customers. I informed him it might be 36, but that I could not say for sure. Of course, Kenneth was perfectly aware that I was at least as cheeky as I was efficient, and because he and I had a really good and solid personal relationship, he accepted the challenge in a positive spirit. Through his strenuous efforts, he managed to boost production. The next year we had found 800 customers hard at work selling Pandora jewelry.

My contact with Pandora primarily took place through Kenneth Ramstrup; my contact with Pandora's other founder, Per Enevoldsen, was more sporadic. Per was the one who had built up Pandora's production facilities in Thailand, and even though our roads rarely crossed, I soon started to feel the spirit Per had helped create in the business. In a great many ways, Kenneth and Per were pretty unique business leaders who were not at all motivated by profit in their approach to doing business.

Sometimes their way of working prompted me to tease them that their business philosophy more or less resembled hard-core communism. To them, it was not just about creating results, but about *how* they created results. Among other things, Per had built a completely unique production facility in Bangkok, Thailand, which supplied jewelry to us distributors. Very quickly I discovered that this factory was, in fact, a kind of heart of the organization: An incredible energy flowed from there, which gradually became an increasingly important asset to both our customers and employees. To bring people down there to see the production universe Per had created in Thailand generated a lot of contagious and extremely positive energy for us who worked proselytizing on behalf of Pandora. When we told our customers that we had a factory in Thailand which produced our jewelry, many imagined rows upon rows of underpaid children laboring away in dismal conditions. It was fantastic to be able to take customers down there to show them the caring way the factory was run. At the factory, Per had created a noticeably Danish working environment where everything took place with the greatest respect for human values and where no one was underpaid or exploited. When we arranged tours of the facilities, we could show that our jewelry was manufactured by a couple of thousand highly-motivated Thai employees who were being treated to all the comforts of life.

During my cooperation with Per, he once invited me to their annual staff party at the Bangkok factory. I have done my share of partying, but I have never experienced anything more dynamic and joyful than what I experienced there. About 3,000 guests had been invited to the party; in the evening, there were performances by some of the most famous Thai musicians and performers. Per was at the center of it all, and he radiated incredible hospitality. Seeing him in the company of his Thai employees, you could clearly feel the respect and love that existed between them. Everyone knew that Per was not just a businessman who created results; he was also someone willing to give his employees everything within his power. For example, it is difficult for most Thais to borrow money the way we do it from banks in our part of the world. Through the company, he had developed a system which enabled his employees to borrow money for such things as cars or houses.

Per's efforts in Thailand had created what I always thought of as the original and genuine Pandora spirit. He showed by example how warmth, kindness, and humanity can be translated into extreme productivity. I took every opportunity to bring people down to meet Per and our employees at our factory. Once you had experienced how our jewelry was produced, you could only love Pandora. One of the reasons I had so much success with Pandora was, no doubt, that not only was the product excellent, I was personally infected by the joy and positive spirit that came from the factory in Thailand. After having visited the facility in Thailand about ten times, I still could not quite figure out how 2,000 happy and smiling people managed to supply us with more than one million pieces of jewelry a week. If I walked into Per's office, he would sit there most of the time looking at four monitors supervising production. Per was the only person who had any idea how everything was interrelated and organized. This is an extraordinarily risky way of running a business: if something would have happened to Per, the entire business would collapse. Because of that, they later trained more people to handle the overall responsibility at the factory.

In the years that followed, Pandora grew at a fantastic speed, and as Pandora grew, the collection not only took Vero Firenze's spot, but knocked it almost completely out of the market. Today, when I look back at those days, spearheading the kind of development we underwent, those years were some of the most exciting of my life. I was in my natural element. Through my work, I had the opportunity to combine everything I had learned and apply it in a constructive process to build up a fantastic organization. With the new Pandora spirit as the wind at our backs, everything I touched turned to gold and everywhere I went orders would pour in at torrential speeds. It was suddenly clear to me that there was no limit to the kind of business I was in the process of creating, and to stand right there in the eye of the hurricane and to help create something of that magnitude was absolutely intoxicating to me. Every day I would get to work and be ready to make tons of decisions, but it was always a matter of making positive decisions. In order to keep the expansion going, I dedicated all my time to motivating as many people as at all possible. I therefore set out creating a great number of events and arrangements where I could talk to customers or meet employees. Soon, more countries were added, and my markets increasingly appeared like a big buffet table where my employees and I could eat as much and as fast as we wanted.

As Pandora was going through this expansion, jewelers told us that their customers had started to ask specifically for jewelry from Pandora. Of course, this sounds like a natural consequence of our success, but in reality this was a kind of revolution in the jewelry industry. For many years, there were these so-called high-end brands, which were jewelry for the wealthy and which cost at least ten times more than it did to manufacture them. No one had really talked about branded goods before as far as jewelry for regular consumers was concerned. But with Pandora's visibility in the market, those days were over. The fact that we succeeded in adding a brand dimension to Pandora not only meant that customers started requesting it specifically, but also that it was important that the product was genuine and not just a copy. In that way, Pandora became more of a product but also a story: where it came from, how it was sold, how it was produced, who did so, and why. That Pandora had now become a brand also made it easier for us to knock copies out of the market. Pandora was Pandora, and even if something resembled Pandora and only cost half as much, it held very little appeal for customers.

In 2006, with Pandora established as a brand, I started to sense that it might be time to open a Pandora Store—in other words, a store that would sell *only* Pandora products. The idea was that our products would no longer be sold as a collection in a store but would be presented on their own, in a completely separate store, as the only product. When I put the idea on the table, no one else thought the time was quite right. Because I was completely alone in this vision, no one was willing to back the idea in my own organization. I had to go out and make that first store a reality myself, have it furnished, and organize our entire strategy around it. When I started, the management team at Pandora became very reluctant; they were afraid that we might upset our jewelers with that kind of initiative. However, this had no impact on my vision, which was not based on strict reasoning but more on a sensation. Even though the sales director at Pandora did not believe in my ideas for the Pandora Store concept, he was still open-minded and willing to make some room for an original idea. He could sense that I had the energy to carry it out, so he told me I was welcome to try. Today, there are slightly fewer than 1,000 Pandora Stores across the world. It is somewhat thought-provoking that I, for the opening of the first store in Hamburg, was responsible for the whole launch. The night before we opened the store, my dad and I were still crawling around on the floor hammering shelves into the wall.

Once an item is endowed with a brand dimension, a number of fresh dynamics are introduced as well as completely different psychological and sales-related mechanisms. It is no longer just a product. If you, as a company, are not the distributor of a brand, it is naturally impossible for you to open a specialty store with products from that same company. If you take, for example, handbags, shoes, or perfume, the market in these segments has been controlled by major brands for many years. In the western world, it has long been difficult to sell a piece of clothing unless it has some kind of brand recognition attached to it. In the clothing industry, you have the major high-end brands, such as Dior, Gucci, Dolce & Gabbana, and Varsity. Then you have a number of more mainstream brands that normal people can afford to buy, such as Boss or Hilfiger. It was this big mainstream segment that was new to the jewelry industry, and because it was created by Pandora, we naturally became the supreme ruler of this segment.

Many have asked me how to create a brand. One way to do it is, of course, to produce ads aimed at your customers. But that kind of branding costs lots of money, and if that is the only way you are going to approach it, you easily risk advertising yourself into an early grave. Of course, you cannot avoid advertising, but my way involved using what I call my *four channels*. Channel 1 was home—that is, Pandora. Here, it was about generating pride in the things we were making and in what our company stood for. We needed all of our employees to agree that the products, the organization, and the community we were creating together were something we could take pride in. At Pandora, this pride gradually became more and more evident to both us and our customers. My employees would often tell me how proud they were when, for example, they booked hotel rooms and told the concierge that they came from Pandora. Once that energy had been established, I turned to Channel 2. Channel 2 concerns our sales representatives who need the ultimate toolbox in the form of high-quality products, marketing materials, service plans, bookkeeping, and all the back office support they could possibly imagine. If the sales reps feel that they are given this kind of support, they will feel fantastic and be 100% ready to deliver a spectacular piece of work. In this way, great energy can be transmitted from Channel 1 to Channel 2. Once you had activated both Channels 1 and 2, the sales rep can then carry that energy out to Channel 3, i.e. the stores. The sales reps must be able to stand in the jeweler's store and talk about his products with an infectious pride, energy, and visibly take great satisfaction in his work. In this way, we can carry the energy on to Channel 3, which would naturally be transmitted to Channel 4, the consumers.

Of course, we cannot simply rely on jewelers talking up Pandora to sustain our sales to consumers. As I mentioned before, if you want to create a brand you do need to advertise your items. In my work with Pandora, I therefore performed a lot of different stunts in the media that created the kind of exposure we needed. For example, at one point I contacted one of the major German fashion magazines and told them I wanted to prepare a supplement for their magazine with 50 pages that *only* dealt with Pandora. The magazine's management was actually pretty shocked and told me that it couldn't be done. "Why not?" I asked. "I'll put together 25 ads about our various products, and you will add some editorial copy on Pandora." Little by little, I succeeded in getting the magazine's management to realize that it was actually a pretty good idea; we set the idea in motion, and they gave me a bill for about $270,000 plus printing costs and everyone was happy. The magazine published 570,000 copies, and it naturally generated tremendous publicity for Pandora, exactly where we needed it.

The next year I decided to go with a different approach. About once a quarter, I had an agency perform a survey of how well-known Pandora was to the general population. The agency would call random people and ask them two types of questions. One type was asking respondents to list whatever jewelry brands they knew. Then, they would flip the question by asking respondents if they knew of Troldekugler, Fossil, Vero Firenze, Pandora, or other brands. When I saw the findings of these surveys, I realized we were growing too slowly. From April to August, awareness of Pandora had only increased from 36 to 38 percent. The cause for this was that I had exhausted the channel I used when I communicated with end consumers. We had already reached readers of fashion magazines or users of the other channels the jewelry business used. Everyone else had no idea what Pandora was. I decided that we needed to do something with television. I sensed that there had to be a very large group of people who watched quite a lot of television but who would never open a fashion magazine. When I broached the idea with my marketing director, he almost fell off his chair. In very clear language, he explained to me that there had *never* been a jewelry brand that had gone on national German television to advertise its products. "Well, then that's precisely what we need to do!" I exclaimed. We then started investigating how that would work, and soon we had three of Germany's biggest media agencies pitch their ideas on how that could be done. The agency we settled on did 600 32-second spots for a period of six weeks—and they all ended with: "Get your starter bracelet at your nearest jeweler!" The price would then flash on the screen in the last couple of seconds. The campaign cost in the neighborhood of $270 million and had a much greater impact than I had expected. Over the six weeks of the campaign, the awareness of Pandora shot up from 38 to 52 percent, and after that, our business went completely crazy.

Another activity that produced an incredible response was a number of road shows where we drove through all the major German cities. These shows were not directed at consumers but were about transmitting the energy to the jewelers that *they* needed to transmit to the consumers; or to put it differently, to transmit energy directly from Channel 1 to Channel 3. Every morning at these road shows, my crew and I would start at a five-star hotel preparing for a show in the evening. In each place, all the area's jewelers were invited for an excellent dinner, after which I would give a talk for a couple of hours on our collection. My German was now at a level which meant I no longer had to scramble around for the right words when I talked. I could therefore perform without PowerPoint slides and a script—just shoot the talk straight from the hip. Each place I made a big deal out of reminding myself that it was exactly in this forum that I might meet my next largest customer. The intention was to have everyone have at least as good an experience as those who had attended the road show the day before. Gradually, these performances developed into a fascinating mixture of equal parts standup comedy, dissemination of facts and figures, and story-telling about Pandora jewelry. I would talk about how the jewelry was produced, how that market had developed, and how and why women were particularly susceptible to the Pandora virus. During the years I performed these shows, I gradually developed many hundreds of stories and punch lines that often occurred to me as I was doing my bit. For instance, I might say that I had never really understood fashion magazines or women. Perhaps it was really just me who had been unlucky, but all the women in my life had had *one* major interest in common: shopping—every single day, if they could get away with it. I might ask my audience if there was anyone there who had either a daughter or a sister who was not interested in shopping. If so, I would love it if they could set me up on a date.

All the topics or themes upon which I based my talk were naturally based on my own experiences with jewelry, business, or the women of significance in my own life. The idea was to give my audience the opportunity to have fun while recognizing themselves in the stuff I was talking about. But I also wanted to speak sincerely about why this was the time to make an extra effort to sell far more Pandora jewelry. When I wrapped up the evening, I was never quite sure how well I had performed. It gave me great peace of mind when my regular crew would tell me afterward that they never tired of hearing my talk. After the talk, we would usually end up in the bar until four in the morning, after which it was time to pack up and move on to the next city.

For everything I did, I took charge and presented myself everywhere I could. I participated in every meeting with store chains and all meetings with major customers, and this made me incredibly visible as an icon and figurehead for Pandora. When I did road shows, I was the host and filled the whole picture. When you do that kind of show for large groups of people for up to 40 days in a row, people start remembering who you are. It also sent a clear signal to my employees that I was never idle, and this would motivate them to show me that they could do something for the company too. If you, as I did, decide to be the CEO and a visible icon, it is paramount that you recognize what kind of person you are and what your temperament is. Some might feel more natural leading their business from the top floor of their headquarters. From there, they can keep a watchful eye on all the key figures and look at efficiency reports and everything else. Our building, too, had a beautiful office—

with designer furniture and other kinds of luxury. At one point, as a joke, my staff had wrapped my office chair in date-stamped paper. The purpose was to see how long it would be before I would be back at the office and would then had to unwrap the chair. When I finally took the paper off my chair to sit in my office, it had been three months since the last time I had been back. When I left Pandora, my staff told me that I had been at the headquarters fewer than ten times since they had opened.

As I continued the expansion in Europe, Kenneth Ramstrup was quick to see the opportunities that were opening up. As they arose, the tools, methods, and the organization I had created became an inspiration to the rest of the organization. On that basis, Kenneth gradually managed to get in touch with some very accomplished people who were able to export Pandora's success to other markets—including Asia and the United States. By showing the world how well things went in Germany, we managed to generate a great deal of trust in Pandora. It was a kind of domino effect as the markets fell one by one, and before long. Pandora was not only big in Europe—it was now a global brand that completely dominated the mainstream segment.

In my approach to the organization, I had full confidence that the whole machinery was running like clockwork and that the people in charge of production and sales knew what they were doing. This confidence is naturally a matter of sensing that things are going well, and if you have that sensation it is a good thing to rely on it. It is said that a good ship's captain can sense if the least little thing is wrong on his ship just by standing on the bridge, feeling the ship's vibrations in his feet. This became my goal—to be able to sense the organization's vibrations and constantly sense that everything was healthy and whether things were going in the right direction. I did this with great success over those years when I managed things up until 2009. When we reached revenues of nearly $300 million, my ship took a new course, and things happened that would have drastic consequences for me personally and for my almost 500 employees.

In Carsten's Words

Bits and pieces

On having tons of money and joining an exclusive club

I'm on my way by car out to Jesper's house by the water, right outside of Copenhagen. I step out of the car and notice a coin on the sidewalk next to my foot. Instinctively, I bend down and pick it up. On my way into Jesper's house, I am wondering whether he would have done the same.

Do you take the time to pick up lost change? I was actually just thinking about that the other day. At the airport, I exited my car and dropped some change, which I spent considerable time picking up. I'm spending a lot of money on things that are completely irrational. But when I see money on the street, I can't just leave it there. In reality, I probably have too much respect for money to leave it on the ground. Afterward, I might remember that—well, ouch, there's my bad back and, wait, this might not be worth my while. Perhaps it will wear out my back so much that I later have to go and get surgery, and then, of course, it would cost quite a lot more in lost wages.

On a broader note, during the period Pandora went through the roof financially, most people were preoccupied with the ongoing financial crisis. If people lack money, you'd think that one of the first things to be cut from the budget would be jewelry. How do you make sense out of the fact that you were able to earn *that* much money during *exactly* that period? I think it has to do with

71

the fact that the financial crisis doesn't interest me. I don't follow the economic climate or macroeconomic trends at all. Everything related to that has no impact on my work principles. Downturns, exuberant times, upturns, or depressing times—I don't care. You'll never hear me talk about the financial crisis as an excuse that I wasn't successful doing something. The financial crisis is, in reality, nothing more than an excuse embraced by inept business people so that they can explain why they aren't successful.

So, you didn't lose money during the financial crisis? Sure I did. I lost a great deal of money on the properties I had bought, but when I buy a property it is because I need it—not because I'm looking to invest money. Therefore, that's not something that worries me terribly. Prices go up and down constantly, and I'm fine with that.

You don't have any stocks or bonds? No, I would never dream of investing in anything like that. The money I earn, I spend on running my business.

Isn't that pretty unusual; that a man like you doesn't invest? Sure, that's why I'm constantly being chased by all kinds of smart bankers who want to tell me how to invest my money in one thing or the other. However, the thing is that I don't have respect for someone who tells me that he became a millionaire by speculating on the stock exchange. You see, he is really more of a lottery millionaire than a businessman. That kind of person has not made a difference for anyone; he has not created jobs; and he doesn't have my respect. To me, it is far more interesting if someone started a small greengrocers that is doing well which injects life into the local community and creates jobs for people who need them.

Are you a member of any forms of business networks? Apart from the parties, events, and arrangements I host, I don't do things like that. To me, things need to have a natural genesis, and if you're registered with some network group under the rubric of "networking," it all becomes far too artificial for me.

But didn't you tell me at some point that you were a member of a network for people with their own jets? Oh, that's true. But, really, it's not much more than a mailing list where we get together for an outing once in a while.

Right now you don't have a jet—does that mean you're off the list? Once you've had your own airplane you're a permanent member of the network. But you also need to bear in mind that I am in the start-up phase with my new company, Endless Jewelry. With the work I'm doing at this particular stage, I don't need an airplane and can get by quite well by just using commercial airlines. But when I need it again, of course, I'll get a private jet.

But do you meet regularly with the people who have their own airplanes? I wouldn't say regularly, but, as I mentioned, we do go out when we get together, or we meet up in airport terminals, shoot the breeze, and tell stories. We all know that everyone on a private jet will have an exciting and completely unique business story, and the story doesn't go away because you can get by using commercial airlines for a while.

Once you've checked in for a regular flight, you risk having to undergo a body search. You are treated like a potential suicide bomber trying to sneak explosives on the plane in your shampoo bottle. I've often wondered what happens when you travel around in the world in your private plane. Well, it's obviously a bit easier.

One of the reasons I don't like flying is the crowded chaos you become part of at the airport. Could you say a few words about the procedure when you have your own airplane? I've gradually become quite familiar with most of the private airports in Europe, and some are easier to use than others. The best one in Denmark is Roskilde Airport, so that's the one I use. When I need to go by plane, I typically send a message to my pilot the moment I leave home. This way he'll know, absent any traffic congestion, that I'll be there 20 minutes later. If suddenly you decide to postpone departure by an hour, that's entirely up to you. For my most recent private jet, I had six permanent pilots which meant that there would always be two ready to take off. Once I arrive, we have our own parking lot—now I come to think of it, I don't think I've ever seen VW Golfs or Audis parked there. Usually, I take my customized Porsche, park it, and throw the key to the staff before being received by the pilot. He then takes my briefcase before we enter the terminal.

You don't go through security? Sure, they x-ray your luggage and send you through a metal detector, but when you travel this way, there is a pretty good and pleasant atmosphere. Then you continue straight out to your plane and you're off. And you can choose where in the world you want to land. From the time I park the car until I'm airborne, it's a matter of less than five minutes, and 20 minutes later I can land in Hamburg or wherever else I'm going. The year Pandora grew at its fastest rate, I made 405 trips in my own jet within 12 months; my all-time record was to lift off seven times in a single day visiting four countries.

So, what do you have to do to get your own jet? Do you buy it and do you own it yourself? It's not like a car where you have to make sure it's inspected, fueled and taken in for service appointments. To get a private jet, you contact a company that handles those kinds of things for you. All they want to know is the size of jet you want and how often you are looking to use it. In my case, I decided to have it available 24 hours a day, 364 days a year. The only day I couldn't use it was on Christmas Eve. The pilots are all off on that day.

Which type of jet did you have? I started with one that wasn't particularly big. But it's like cars and boats. They tend to get bigger and bigger. Most recently, I had one with big club seats and my own kitchen. But I also thought that there was an upper limit for the size of jet I really needed. For my part, I only needed to fly within Europe and that greatly influenced my choice of model. One of my friends who often flew back and forth between Europe and the United States teased me for having what he called a discount jet and having to share a toilet with my pilots when we were airborne.

On a different subject, almost all self-respecting businesses are busy defining their values and corporate mission statements. In our conversations, I haven't really heard you mention that kind of stuff, Why? I've never seen any need to waste my time or that of my employees with defining mission and value statements. The question is why you would want to set values that you know will never be adhered to anyway. In many companies, they spend days trying to find a few words—such as, for example, "trust," "pride," or "quality"—only to go back to business as usual. I think I saw somewhere that J.P. Morgan's values statement says something like "We perform to the highest standards for our clients and shareholders." I mean, honestly, give me a break! What does that even mean? The values we have in KASI Group are not something we have defined but something that is just there. We don't need to advertise it to the general public. In fact, I've never given our values a great deal of thought. But if I were forced to define our three most important values, they'd be: "Fun," "fun," and "fun"— or to put it differently: It has to be a blast to go to work!

I've noticed you're pretty preoccupied with having fun and partying. That coupled with your unorthodox views on doing business—I guess a natural question would be if you've ever taken drugs. Have you? Er, it is pretty widely known that I am pretty wild at parties, but, with respect to drugs, I'm the most boring person imaginable. Throughout my entire life, I have never even taken a single drag on a cigarette. I would also never dream of drinking beer or wine. I just don't like the taste. My employees and customers often laugh at me because I'm so prehistoric: I prefer rum and Coke but rarely in such quantities that I get drunk.

If I were to describe my relationship with drugs or alcohol, I'd say that you could describe my condition as being "high on life"—that is, to live and apply myself to whatever I'm good at. That's the only drug I am hooked on.

I'm aware that you have sometimes had some confrontations with your banks. Could you elaborate, in general terms, on your relationship with banks? In recent years we have seen a great number of banks that have tanked. One of the reasons is that at the very top of the financial world, there are people with unlimited opportunities to borrow money. This means that bank doesn't put enough thought into whether a business is sustainable. And this harms regular people or the small entrepreneurs who have a difficult time borrowing money. For that reason, I could very easily imagine a scenario where, in ten years, I would start a bank for entrepreneurs with good projects.

So, how would you know if a project is any good? Generally, the quality of a project is not so much about the product you are trying to launch. What decides whether a project or a business can be successful is more often about whether the person who is trying to launch it is willing to put skin in the game. If you ask most entrepreneurs if they are ready to mortgage their home to the hilt, be away from their family for six months a year, or work 24 hours a day, you'll quickly see people scratching their heads. A good project is always built on 100 percent dedication.

Has it ever occurred to you that your mentality might seem a little strange for many of the people around you? Some people are just born into the wrong time or place

where they don't fit into the culture in question. I guess my question is where you, culturally, belong. Funny you should say that. One of my American friends often tells me that I'm more American than most Americans. According to him, I should pack my bags immediately and go to the United States. To him, there is no doubt whatsoever that I would thrive over there. Many Europeans see Americans as superficial, but many of them seem to me to be incredibly honest, generous, and unpretentious. That style suits me very well.

Do you feel inhibited being in a culture—like the Danish one—where many see you as not really fitting in? In the beginning it did. But at one point I realized that it would only inhibit me if I didn't fully stand by who I am. You can't listen to just half of your gut feeling or only stand by what you are, in part. It doesn't work like that. To me, you either need to have a façade or leave it out altogether. In established business life, there is a certain culture where you dress a certain way, speak a certain way, etc. etc. Instead of putting yourself on a pitch others have created, I make sure to chalk out my own pitch. And once we're on my pitch, it's not difficult to push an opponent out of the game.

Could you point to some of the problems you've experienced because you don't fit into the Danish culture in particular? Generally, I feel that people around me start to focus more on me as a person rather than what we need to accomplish together. Once in a blue moon, I've felt that kind of focus in an employee who starts taking offense at the way I'm living my life. Those kinds of issues can be difficult to address. It usually means that I need to close down and get rid of the person in question as soon as possible.

What would you say is the most important element in creating a successful organization? The ability to make quick decisions. I often visit companies where I see 20 people with very long and complicated job descriptions, who are doing tons of stuff that, when push comes to shove, is completely irrelevant. You could eliminate everything those people are doing by just making a number of quick decisions about whether the business should go in one direction or the other. If you make many quick decisions, sure, you'll make mistakes once in a while. But those mistakes will always be outweighed by the increased efficiencies that have resulted from daring to make decisions. When someone asks me something, they will always get a quick and very specific answer. That is effective leadership and that is what yields results.

Do you have a business philosophy? Yes. My philosophy is that my default position will be to say yes to everything. "Yes" is a positive answer and that is the attitude we want to have. I always teach my employees that if they're interacting with a customer, they need to say yes to everything. Generally, customers will always have a lot of expectations and demands that may seem peculiar. As a business you try to make their demands and expectations a part of what you offer. With me, it has always been a matter of principle that no matter what customers are requesting, they will get a yes. If what the customer requests is impossible, i.e. it is not our lack of will that is the problem but when what he or she has requested really, *really* cannot be done. While I worked with Pandora, I had such experiences many times. Perhaps I would have a customer telling me that they wanted their gift boxes in a different size and color because their town had just celebrated its 500th anniversary. Of course I would always say yes to that kind of stuff. It would usually not take long before I would have a cranky brand manager on the phone complaining that we are not complying with the rules in our brand book. My answer is always that I really couldn't care less about the brand book. Our most important task is to make sure we have a satisfied customer on our hands who won't forget the kind of pampering we gave him. My very *least* concern, frankly, is whether or not the person fiddling with the brand book is happy or unhappy—we shouldn't be limited by the guidelines he sets. The only brand book I need is the one between my ears, and it couldn't be clearer: The customer will get what the customer wants. You know, there is nothing easy about a "yes." The easiest answer you can give a customer or business partner is a "no," because a "no" means that you have not committed yourself to do anything. But if you say "yes," you actually have to get busy, and I guess that's why we're there.

But if you never say "no," don't you end up with no boundaries at all? Sure, and naturally we're not going say "yes" if the customer asks if he or she can have the item at half price. But setting those kinds of rules is something you need to do with such clear conviction that the customer would never dream of asking that question. If you have established a presence with your customers and if you know what you're doing and where you're headed, there are, of course, a lot of questions it would never even occur to them to ask. One of these questions is whether or not they can have a discount. Almost everywhere, people are incredibly preoccupied with the price of the things they produce—not me. When I set the price for an item, I never calculate that price based on being able to provide discounts but on being able to provide excellent service. When selling jewelry, I might gather three of Germany's competitors in the industry at the same meeting. Normally, of course, you just don't do that kind of thing. But I can because all three will have *exactly* the same financial agreement with me.

So, perhaps that's the explanation why so many of your customers find it so easy to work with you? I think one of the reasons I have always been very popular with my customers is that it's easy for them to see who I am.

Then, perhaps, you could tell me a bit more about who you are? Quite simply: I'm just a regular guy selling regular jewelry to regular people for regular money. Many people who haven't met me before think that they are about to meet some supremely arrogant jewelry king. But when we finally sit down face to face, they often make a point of pointing out to me that I am the most understanding and flexible person they've ever met. Ever since I started working at gas station marts as a very young man, I have always had the same attitude—and that is that *anything* is possible! It produces enormous respect when you have transacted business with each other, and the customer can tell that you always listen and always understand and because you are constantly doing all you can do to find a solution that makes the customer happy.

Stunt No. 3

Drop the résumé

On hiring people based on gut feeling

As everyone who knows me is aware, I am not highly educated and I do not express myself in academic terms. My background is my high school education, and as far as business is concerned, I have a fundamental knowledge about business processes and about how you put together a balance sheet and profit/loss and cash flow statements. And, I am pretty good at doing arithmetic in my head. Naturally, there have been times when I wondered if I should get a business degree. It might be interesting as an academic exercise, but I have just never been able to see what use it would be to me. At school, teachers would often compliment me on my problem-solving skills, but school just never really interested me. I would much rather work at a gas station mart and deal with real down-to-earth challenges. To me, it was fantastic to experience all the different people streaming through that kind of store on a daily basis. I could usually remember people's names after only seeing their faces and running their credit cards once. In short, my approach to things is completely practical and is everything but theoretical—and it has had a profound influence on how I conduct interviews with people. For example, I do not waste my time looking at someone's résumé before I hire him or her. When you are holding that résumé in your hand, you do not really see much more than how many hours the author used in setting up his story in a smart tabulated system and making it look as if he or she can do tons of stuff. The only problem is that I could not care less in knowing anything about how a person *wants* to appear; I do not want to feel manipulated by the gloss they have put on their lives. When you are sitting across from someone who will be helping you on critical projects, become a part of a team, and accomplish big things, I only need to know a single but very important question: "Who are you *really*?"

If I were legally permitted to do so, I would prefer to have all important job interviews in the interviewee's home. In that way I could see how they live, how they arrange their lives, what their priorities are, and meet their kids and significant others to get a feeling of what kind of person he or she really is that I am about to invite into my business. It is in a person's private life you get a true picture of who that person really is—something I know from my own experience. If you visited me at the KASI House, you would experience a very clean and stylistically beautiful environment. But if you visit me today, at my *real* home, you would see that everything is a mess with toys and kids' shoes strewn about everywhere. In my private home, there is a side of me who believes it is okay to be surrounded by chaos—a side that takes up a lot of space and that you would not discover until you got closer to me. Your home tells a story about what it takes for you to feel relaxed and to let go, whereas the glossy version presented on your résumé will show the kind of person you want other people to think you are. That is why I have completely dropped the idea of looking at résumés but instead hire people based on only two criteria. One is *personality*, the other is *attitude*. This means that I could not care less what they did before they reach my office. And quite often, I have been in situations where I have hired new key employees without asking a single question about that person's academic or professional history. For example, we might have four different interviews or discussions where I sense that everything is in perfect order. If everything turns out *not* to be in perfect order, and it turns out that I have hired a person who has been playing with a stacked deck, I always find out within the first three months. Regardless of the caliber of actor he or she is, it is always those first three months that are decisive. And if I cannot manage to get under that façade within that period, I can conclude that there is no façade, and everything is usually in perfect order.

In other words, whether or not my interviewees were elected class president, valedictorian, homecoming queen, or "best employee of the month" 20 years in a row is irrelevant to me. Because I am bold enough to seek out other types of qualities in people, I sometimes find diamonds others would never find. That is why the questions and themes we broach during an interview might be about anything else than what most people are prepared to talk about. I generally prefer to talk about whether an applicant is good at sports, what the applicant wants to be when he or she grows up, if he or she is any good at partying, and if the applicant likes being drunk, or other themes along those lines. If you are seeking employees who are going to move mountains for you, it is critical that they have the stamina—and if there is something I do not like, it is hiring managers who, just when the party gets going, need to leave to be in bed by 10:30. Such parties are all about being able to hang around in the bar until four in the morning with your customers or employees, but also about being ready for meetings the next day and be ready to go by 8:00 a.m. People who need to go to bed early to be able to get up at 6:30 a.m. to go jogging, before spending a lot of time putting on their face, do not fit into my business model. Those kinds of people often fail to comprehend that it is in the bar in the evening and at night that the great connections or big transactions are made. Maybe they go into the first meeting of the morning, fresh and looking like a million bucks—and we need to give it a bit extra because we are not feeling all that great. The only difference is that, after having spent the night in the bar, you have created relationships—they have not. The moment you have been "under the influence" with some-one, you have something to build: We have allowed our-selves to show sides of each other that are more straight-forward and open than if we had been sober. If you have reached that point in a relationship, you have created some-thing that is more honest and genuine than what you can create in a conference room. It is only when you have cast a solid and honest foundation that you can start building great things together.

Naturally, I am aware that alcohol can get out of control and does not always bring out the best in people. But I also see how drinking and partying can get people to open up in every way. This is a contributing reason that my company most likely has something approaching a world record in creating sweethearts. To get a lot of employees together in a hotel, get them drunk and party until four in the morning invites all kinds of openness, but also all kinds of problems. Whether or not people are good at handling that kind of stuff and whether they can get something nice out of it is not something you can assess based on their education, their résumés, their references as employee of the month, or whatever else they may choose to show or tell you at a job interview. The higher a person's level of education, the bigger my problems are later on in the process. What I need is the ability to handle openness, combined with the capacity to perform from morning to evening.

With respect to my approach to recruiting new employees, my methods have been unorthodox over the years. For example, I walk around with a stack of business cards in my pocket and hand them to people I meet who provide good service. If I go to a bakery and meet a person I like, he or she will get a business card, and I will tell them: "I've no idea what you can do or what your background is, but based on the way you have just served me, I'd like to hire you. So if you ever need a different job, feel free to contact me."

Of course, I am primarily spending my time hiring managers, and the people I have hired naturally also need to be able to do arithmetic and write. But that is pretty much where the significance of a formal education stops for me. The message I generally try to convey to managers is that, of course, it is a bonus if they are smart and if they have created results before they came to the interview. But unless their colleagues or staff like them, we will have to part ways again. I should be able to go to the manager's colleagues and ask them if they like their supervisor, and they need to be able to look me in the eyes and let me know that they like him or her. If the general consensus is that a manager does not have the emotional support of his or her colleagues, we will part ways quite quickly.

Another central aspect of my strategy with regard to my employees is to combat gossip. In major companies, enormous resources are spent on people gossiping, creating rumors, or otherwise creating noise, which means that they are never getting anywhere. Gossip is one of the efficient organization's greatest enemies, and in all the organizations where I have been responsible, gossip is dismissal cause number 1. This is something I always make clear to new people before hiring them. The moment you start speaking evil about others in the business, you have signed your own walking papers. To me, it is critical to practice the old virtue: "If you have nothing nice to say about others, keep your mouth shut!" Many people have asked me over the years why I only have good things to say about my colleagues or customers. Why not? My reply is quite simple: If I did not have good things to say about them, there would be no reason to spend such a large part of my life with them.

Stunt No. 4

Be your own coach

On not attending personal development seminars and finding answers for yourself

When I hire people, it is generally based on my sense of them as I am talking to them. In my way of thinking, people are relatively static entities which I cannot do much to change. If we are talking about staff members that do not fit into their workplace, I often see it as the best option for everyone to just part ways rather than trying to move or motivate them with courses and discussions, etc. Obviously, you might actually find that a colleague gets something out of a seminar or becomes capable of making minor adjustments to his or her behavior after a long series of development interviews. But a course will not prompt an employee to undergo such major changes that he or she will change her life or outlook on his or her job. Change is something you experience when you are tripped up by life or when you go out and meet new people—not by attending a carefully planned course.

If you want to be part of the so-called corporate world—and I know I am probably stepping on quite a few toes here—forget about leadership development, personal development, and coaching. To me, they seem like a pure waste of time and money. If you look closely at the participants who attend courses in, for example, leadership development, you will soon discover that what they are mostly focused on is what hotel they will be staying at, what fancy cuisine they will be trying in the evenings, and if there is going to be partying and drinking at night. I am not saying that leadership development courses do nothing; no one can attend a course without getting *something* out of it. But bear in mind, when you go out for drinks with your buddies, you are also getting something out of it—you do not need a structured environment for that. In my previous career as regional manager of the supermarket chain, I was forced to go on an exclusive leadership seminar that all the managers had to attend. Not only was it *incredibly* expensive; it was also totally career-breaking. The course featured a number of collaborative exercises where some former Special Forces soldiers had us rappelling down structures, building bridges over creeks, and similar activities. At one of the exercises, one of our really capable managers tripped, fell down, and was injured so badly that she was never able to work again. All I could think of was *not* how well we had overcome obstacles, but what a waste of time and potential, what was the sense of arranging such an extreme course, and what good would actually come of it?

During this so-called leadership development course, we were also asked to commune with nature. Among other things, we had to talk to an old Native American, stare into a tree for six hours, and emit primal screams. If you did not give it your all, you were accused of not being willing to open up. What no one talked about was whether or why you actually really *needed* to be open or participate in any of these absurd processes. Supposedly, it was to learn the importance of being able and willing to change—to embrace freedom. But to me, freedom in itself can never be a goal. In reality, freedom is a state that can end up confining a person who is unable to administer his freedom: When a team of former Special Forces soldiers, without empathy and emotional insight, push people into a process like this, they very easily tamper with a lot of stuff they should probably have left alone and create reactions that do far more damage than good. During the course in question, many of the participants fell apart, completely or in part, after which they decided that they either needed a divorce or a different job. The question here is: How on earth is it in the interest or profitable for a company to spend its money helping its employees reach those kinds of conclusions.

Once the course was over, several of my team members behaved as if they had joined a cult. Some started carrying around a dream catcher; others would wear only red jackets; others again, would keep their own little special rock that they could talk to and all other weird kinds of stuff. That is okay, and it is not because I do not think being open is a good idea. But I prefer things to be more authentic. And it is naturally completely absurd that a company would pay a double monthly salary to send their employees on those kinds of excursions. In my eyes, there is no reason for picking people apart or pushing them out so far that they lose their footing. For what? So they can return to work to create change for change's sake?

Now, I started this chapter by saying that you cannot attend a course without bringing something back from the experience. This is naturally true, and what I brought back from that course was my conviction that I would never ever run a single leadership development program in my future career.

All I do is create lots of experiences, parties, and great fun. Through the activities I have arranged, I have personally witnessed that my employees have grown; they have been happy and felt like giving it their all to grow the company. If, for example, I have four employees today that need personal development and team building, the last thing I would dream of would be to send them on a course. Instead, I would rather send them on a boozer for four days to a ski sports resort. It is both less expensive, more effective, and it gives each person the opportunity to set his or her own limits and make his or her own choices about what that person feels like or does not feel like doing. To me, human growth is brought about by having the time to reflect and speak with each other honestly. On that basis, I do not think there is any better team building exercise than renting a six-person van and sending them off to a cottage with the van full of beer or wine. After that kind of trip, you will have created deep relationships, you will have prepared some good food, gone hiking, and talked about whatever you felt like talking about. In many ways, building relationships is really not a big magic trick. Reaching the kinds of levels where we are talking therapy or peer pressure is not at all necessary to get people to perform at their maximum—on the contrary.

Another aspect of what is called business development has to do with coaching. Throughout my entire career, I have never used a coach and never will. Sometimes I am asked: "But does that mean you don't have any problems at all?" Of course I have problems. And when they arise, I will either chat with my friends or make sure I get a good night's rest and then think about how I need to approach the problems in the morning. You need to bear in mind that there is always only *one* person who really knows what your problems are and how they should be resolved, and that is *you*. If you are faced with a problem, you are the only person who has the full picture. And if you are constantly seeking out help and advice from people who do not have the full picture, you are bound to be led in the wrong direction. The more dependent you become on other people to solve your problems, the more difficult it will be to solve your problems yourself. A coach can naturally offer certain angles and perspectives on problems. But since it always you who will end up solving your problems, you might as well try to get better at handling things yourself. That is why I do not need a coach, and I would be surprised if any of my colleagues told me one day that they needed a coach.

Some years ago, I had an employee who was very politically correct, through and through, and who would regularly tell me how he had developed himself through counseling with his coach. I finally managed to poke a hole through his façade, and he finally admitted that the whole thing about the coach had been a white lie. He had just always wanted to send a signal that he was dedicated to personal growth and had settled on that particular story.

Personal growth is nothing you can find, cultivate, or create by attending a seminar. It has nothing to do with sitting in a room for hours doing exercises. Personal growth is something that occurs naturally and organically when you live your life—when you are with your family or when you are with your colleagues at work. When I need to grow personally, I go out and visit my customers. They will give me all the personal growth I need. That is where I will get a sense of what I need to learn and where I need to go. There is no better place to grow.

To round off these thoughts on personal growth, I should also mention that in business, there are an abundance of words that often cover pretty much the same condition. There is talk of leadership growth, team building, personal growth, and personal development and so on and so forth. As mentioned, I regard those kinds of activities as more or less superfluous, but this does mean that I distance myself from people actually seeking therapy. The thing is that seeking therapy is a completely personal issue and is nothing that management should be forcing on its employees. If a person has been exposed to violence in their lives, there is no doubt that it can be a very good thing for that person to open up and either talk about it or examine various nuances. If you have that kind of stuff in your subconscious, it is not only you that you might harm. You might also create a lot of problems for the people around you. I do not personally need therapy, presumably because I had an unusually safe and wonderful childhood—but I can completely empathize with people going through stuff like that.

Stunt No. 5

No tie and jacket

On ignoring dress codes but still minding how you dress

Corporations sometimes seem obsessed with defining various dress codes. It has been drilled into generations that the preferred corporate attire is a jacket, tie, starched shirt, and polished black shoes. Perhaps because I take such issue with conforming, I have always told my employees and others around me that we will do things our way and never try to present ourselves as something we are not. With respect to myself, I am basically just a big, happy boy who likes to have a good time. I tend to see work as just another exciting way to meet a lot of different people. That is who I am and that is reflected in my way of dressing. I try to be remain as authentic as possible and thereby make it as easy as possible for others to relate to me as a person. It was not always like that. Earlier in my career, to blend in, I would most often just dress as convention would have it. This approach to my attire was changed abruptly when I met my present girlfriend in 2004. One day she looked in my wardrobe and asked me where on earth my clothes came from. She had noticed that almost none of my clothes reflected me as a person. She started equipping me with some smart jeans, sneakers, and a sweatshirt, and as soon as I started wearing those things, I suddenly felt much more relaxed. I also stopped looking at what everyone else was wearing to try to figure out how I should dress. And I have dressed whatever

way I want to dress ever since; regardless of where I am going or whom I am meeting.

If you need to wear a freshly pressed and starched shirt to
send the signal that you are a perfect human specimen, we
are talking about a façade. There are no perfect people, so I
will always try to mine what is honest, authentic, and joyful
in people—also with respect to attire. Even as I have given
my colleagues complete freedom to dress any way they
want, there are nevertheless many who decide to stick with
what has long been regarded as the traditional corporate
"uniform." When on business trips around Germany, I am
often been surrounded by employees in traditional business
outfits. Two guys I had hired from a very conservative supermarket chain were especially entrenched in that culture,
which they had been part of their entire careers. After
working for me for some time, I nevertheless gradually
managed to get them to take off their ties. Still, they would
insist on buttoning the top button on their shirts. Once in a
while, I would jokingly go over to them, gently nudge open
their top buttons and tell them it was time to relax and take
it easy. Half an hour later, there they were—their top buttons re-buttoned. When I traveled around with the two of
them, sometimes people were confused if I, or one of them,
was the boss. Standing next to them, I looked like a regular
laborer dragged in off the street.

With respect to my attire, however, there is a different dimension not many people notice. Even if, on the surface,
my attire might look very casual and laid-back, you
would—if you have an eye for those kinds of things—see
that it is not. The sneakers I am wearing cost north of

$1,300. My jeans are from the most hip jeans store in Hamburg. Some of the people who meet me for the first time sometimes want to see if my watch is a genuine Rolex. The fact is that a Rolex would never fit a guy like me. Rolex is the watch you wear if you want to show people around you that you have truly made it and that you have earned a truckload of money. If you need to send those kinds of signals, you are only making it abundantly clear that you are, in fact, not the least bit in control. Watches happen to be one of those things I am really interested in, and one of the most important things to me is that the watches I wear should be limited editions. Only 25 copies of the watch I am wearing right now, for example, were ever produced. It is manufactured by a company called Jaeger-LeCoultre and costs more than what most people earn in a year.

With respect to attire, for me, it is about sending a signal to the general population about who I am but also to be recognized by the people who have reached the same step on the economic ladder as I have. One of the places where you can be sure to meet people who are able to see that my attire is not arbitrary or completely casual is in private airports. With the people there, I am part of a so-called network community where we will always recognize each other by the relaxing but exclusive attire when we meet outside the airports. In a private airport, you never see anyone who enters or exits an airplane with a tie and a jacket. In your career, if you have reached the point where you can spend several million dollars a year on maintaining your own airplane, you no longer need to show the world who you are by wearing a jacket, tie, and polished shoes. In those kinds of places, this would be seen as definite proof that, purely in career terms, you have not yet arrived.

However, there are situations where I might feel a bit of pressure to dress differently. If one day I were to be invited for dinner with the royal family, I would be in a bit of a pickle. In Germany, there are also situations where I have attended major award shows and have been surrounded by hundreds of men all wearing jackets and ties. In those kinds of places, not very many people would be able to appreciate that I am not as casually dressed as it appears. And that is why my attire has often developed into a bit of theme. But attire is not a religious question for me. In reality, your attire is nothing but a surface. But that surface also happens to be the factor that sends the clearest signal of what is hiding underneath. In my case, we are talking about a regular guy but also a bit of a joker. That is why I have regularly decided to shock my surroundings by suddenly showing up as a spectator at a soccer match dressed in tails, top hat, and a white bow tie.

Even if I, over the course of my career, have spent a great deal of money on luxury items and like top-quality products, to me, wealth or luxury has never been a goal in itself. Actually, I tend to live a pretty simple life, and I love taking my family and kids on trips in an old RV and living in relatively primitive conditions. With respect to the luxury that has been an important element in pampering my employees, we do not indulge every day when we are out there earning money. For example, some years ago I hired an extremely competent marketing director. Along with him and two of my old directors, we were going to Bangkok to have some meetings with our manufacturer. The only thing we had agreed on was which flight to take—but we each booked our own tickets. When we arrived at the airplane and entered the cabin, the two old directors walked to the right to go down to steerage. When I arrived at the door, I followed them but was stopped by our new marketing director who was headed to the left to go into business class. Slightly shaken, he asked why we were headed into tourist class. I told him that the trip was paid by the company so there was no reason to squander money. During the time he was my employee, he never flew business class again. Even though I have had my own plane, flying has always been a practical function for me—it has never been about maintaining a certain lifestyle. To fly on business class is something I do only if there are no other seats left on the plane, or if I am going somewhere with my girlfriend and want to spoil her. I feel the same way about hotels. Throughout the years, I have lived in many of the finest hotels in Europe, but if I can manage to get back home to my own bed, I would much rather drive or fly, even if it takes several hours. Regardless of how luxurious a hotel is, the fact remains that thousands of strangers have been sweating on the mattress, using the same linens. Maybe I am a bit sensitive, but for me, luxury is not about what something costs but about whether it makes me relax.

Stunt No. 6

Avoiding pedestals

On reaching pinnacles and keeping it real

Of all the people that have worked for me throughout my entire career, I have never experienced any of them resigning unless I personally wanted to get rid of them. In other words, I have never had a single employee who has approached me and told me that he or she had found a different company where they would rather work. The reason this would not occur to them is because they have been working in a company where they have felt both that their hard work was appreciated and that there was room for growth, in human as well as in professional terms. In order to be able to give the people around you the space and opportunities to grow, there are a number of preconditions that need to be in place first. In KASI Group, I was the supreme authority, founder, and owner. When you are in that kind of position in relation to your staff, you have quite a great deal of power. However, exercising power can easily become a situation where you end up putting a person in a window and airless box and take away his or her opportunities to develop. I usually say that the more power you have, the more careful you need to be not to use it. To refrain from using power to put people in boxes has, in my own career, been something that has grown gradually more challenging.

When KASI Group underwent its explosive growth, I was elevated to a higher and higher plateau and that made it more and more difficult to maintain close contact with individual staff members. This created a certain distance between my employees and me, which felt very overwhelming when we finally did manage to meet face to face. Many of my employees reacted by elevating me into some kind of idol, which meant that they reacted with a kind of weird reverence when I would contact them. Some people might feel a certain discomfort by having other people listening to your every word and prostrate themselves in admiration of the decisions you make. I really don't like that, and the first time I sensed that someone reacted in that manner, I felt an instinctive resistance. That is why I was also very alert to the fact that the respect for authority that arose around me as KASI Group was growing and could easily become a drag on me and my company. A leader who locks his employees into boxes instead of giving them free rein is in serious trouble. To me, it is all about trying to shorten the distance between my staff and me, to kick over the pedestal, remove the reverence, and try to find a path to a more authentic interaction.

Many people have experienced that sometimes they have difficulty motivating others to do what is asked of them. Because of my place in my own company, where I was the owner, founder, and uncontested leader, it almost became the other way around. I gradually had to pay more and more attention to how forceful I came across—and had to make sure that they did not become too enthusiastic or lose themselves. If I did not hold back a bit, I could well become the direct cause of my staff's losing contact with reality. Before I started realizing I was doing this when I held meetings or talked to groups, I would sometimes start riffing on a topic I did not quite believe in myself. And then, as I got going, I would sometimes gradually convince myself that what I was talking about was, in fact, the case. When I talked to a group of people, I would often go off on a tangent and speak on that. At the start, it may just have been a stray thought, an idea, or a sensation, and as I was talking about it and explaining it, it developed into something bigger and bigger. If, during this process, I did not pay sufficient attention to whether I was talking based on actual reality or just my sensation of what seemed real, problems would arise. Those kinds of situations can be pretty risky if you are not paying very close attention. If you have psychopathic tendencies, you might end up seducing your listeners instead of motivating, encouraging, or inspiring them. That is why, today, I try to stay on the straight and narrow and focus more on keeping an eye on myself than on the people around me.

That people can lose themselves and be seduced if they have elevated others to be their idols has always been difficult for me to understand. Throughout my life, I have met many people I have admired for what they have accomplished or what they have created, but I have never experienced performance anxiety or lost myself if we have come face to face. When you start idolizing a person, you are effectively creating a distance from that person. And when that distance arises, you not only lose yourself but also the opportunity to take real joy in that other person. If I were to pick one person who has inspired me beyond measure, I would say Richard Branson. This guy is an adventurous daredevil who, among other things, has tried to fly around the world in a hot air balloon, but he is also an incredible business-man who has started a great number of exciting businesses. One of the more thrilling projects Branson has hatched is Virgin Galactic. It is nothing less that the world's first space program targeting tourism. I mean, just imagine that! Branson's people have developed an airplane that can fly 3,700 miles an hour, which means that it can go 62 miles into space to give its passengers the experience of being astro-nauts. To get into the program, you need to undergo exten-sive training and naturally be in top physical shape before the launch. Within the next few months, I will be attending a meeting to hear more about the program—and as soon as possible, I will be off.

One of the first things I ever read about Branson was that he had bought his own island, which he used whenever he needed to indulge his employees. The island is in the trop-ics, and his guests can play golf and tennis in absolutely heavenly surroundings. When I read about that, I had al-ready started my own place in Mallorca and thought it was incredibly inspiring to read his thoughts on the steps he had taken. Personally, I somehow had never really been able to find the right words for why I had started my place, but Branson more than compensated for this. He completely crystallized my ideas. I have devoured all of his books: Here is a man who is a complete visionary, bold enough to think incredibly big. I connect with his worldview which has con-vinced me that my particular path is the right one. Because I go so much against the grain of the established corporate culture, it has been uplifting to partake in his worldview, his way of thinking about business, and his thoughts on creating business while also treating people with respect and kindness.

Stunt No. 7

Let go of the artificial

On being genuine and on being yourself in meetings

Because I have often made mistakes, my accountants or other structured people have sometimes told me: "We need to get somebody onto your board who can manage you!" The only problem is that the moment I let myself be managed, I can quite easily lose what is unique. If I become too limited or too boxed in, I will lose the part of myself that can create and cultivate what is unique. With my organizational approach, I have always paid great attention to things not becoming too technical or too streamlined.

A good example of this is my instinctual aversion to what they call CRM systems. The abbreviation stands for Customer Relationship Management and is about creating a system where you have full control of all of your data on your customers and other people your business deals with. Faced with those kinds of systems, I ask myself the simple question: Why? Stuff you pour into a system like that is nothing but sterile data about people, and controlling your data has nothing to do with being able to succeed in a commercial transaction or a friendship. In order to be able to trade or be friends, data is not what is central. What *is* important is that you have the right energy, openness, presence, and empathy. If these things are in place, you can choose to bond through a transaction or a friendship. If you fill the relationship between people with sterile data, there is no longer any room for a personal relationship. If I started getting people on my company's board who would "manage me," these might easily be people who would waste my time trying to introduce CRM systems or similar nonsense. When I meet someone trying to sell me a CRM system, I usually tell them I already have one, and it is right between my ears. If I do not personally remember something important about other people, it is likely because the person in question is no longer important to me.

Some time ago, I was called up by one of my former customers who invited me to a soccer game in London. The match he had managed to get tickets for meant an enormous amount to him, and I naturally knew everything about that. Additionally, I knew how much it meant to him that *I* should watch that match with him. The fact that we could meet up in London, eat a great dinner, and see the match together will create something between us that will never disappear. And, because we can manage a way to do that, completely without the use of a CRM system, it becomes an infinitely greater experience. With respect to our business connection, I am naturally aware that he is a good customer. Even if we are not necessarily doing a deal the day we are watching the soccer match, there is hardly any doubt that we will be doing a deal at some point. When we meet at the soccer match, I do not give any thought at all to what we will be doing in the future. Here, it is only our meeting and what we are doing together that are important. That we have managed to meet without computers telling us that it was a good idea is exactly part of the strength of this meeting. Human relationships are something that cannot and should not be formalized and automated.

When someone has tried to sell me a CRM system, the sales pitch is often that I can just enter my customers' data. The system will then remind me if a customer's spouse has a birthday and the name of his or her dog. I sometimes get birthday greetings from others where I can sense that their so-called "greeting" *screams* that the sender has acquired a CRM system. In this Facebook age, many have experienced suddenly receiving a "Happy birthday!" from someone they have not spoken to for six months or more. That kind of stuff usually make me want to vomit, because it is crystal clear that this greeting is not based on a person's feelings, which means that there is no reason to pay any attention to it. If the person who sent the birthday greeting had genuinely felt it, if their greeting had come from his or her heart, that person might also have contacted you on dates when it was not your birthday. By creating a system intended to develop relationships, you lose contact with what is authentic, and in truth, you lose contact with each other. Quite apart from that, I should also mention that I have otherwise never been particularly preoccupied with people's birthdays. For all my relationships outside my family, birthdays are completely irrelevant. To me, a birthday is a private event that you can choose to celebrate with your closest relatives. To eat cake with candles and sing birthday songs for my employees are something I would never dream of. I will happily take my business partners or employees to a great party, but to use their birthdays as the reason for this is an unusually bad idea. I would not buy more products from a supplier just because he sent me a CRM-generated birthday greeting—on the contrary. By using a system to send me a greeting, that person only shows that he or she is not taking our relationship seriously and why would I do business with that kind of person?

A good relationship can form the basis for doing business or cultivating friendships. To me, it is all about your capacity to relate at a personal level to others. The stuff you remember about other people and what they remember about you is a natural part of the space you create together. The guy who invited me to London to see a soccer match is a good example of this. As I mentioned, I have no plan to sell him stuff when we meet this time around. But if I have something I want to sell him in, say, six months or three years, we will have skipped the sales situation, and he will not need to ask me all sorts of questions—all he will ask me is when he might be able to buy my products. When trust has been forged at the human level, things happen by themselves, regardless of whether it is about friendship or business.

Life Story Part 2

Best in the world

On leading an obscure sports club to the world cup

Sports have always been very important to me and my family. If there is something we business people love, it is to live out our competitive genes by seeing our favorite team win. The sports world has something the world of business lacks: immediate and clear resolution. In other words, once a sports match is over, you will be able to see who won or lost. In a league tournament, you can always look up scores and see where you are in relation to your competitors. You do not have that in the business world where—with respect to results—things can be pretty murky.

As mentioned, I caught the sports bug early in childhood. I played both soccer and handball, and as the Danish soccer club Brøndby IF started to flourish in the mid-80s and became a top club with impressive international results, I started really following their matches. Even though Brøndby IF was one town over from where I grew up, I was still close enough to be considered a local, and they were, truth be told, not my favorite team in the beginning. But as they became such a supremely skilled team, I started really following them, and as time went by, I would become more and more of a fan. My family and I started going to a few of their matches; this gradually became a regular tradition where we would go out for dinner before watching Brøndby IF play. When my sales activities increased in Germany, my family started having more money to spend. We decided to take out a small sponsorship in Brøndby IF and spend some of our money to make Brøndby IF a gathering point for our business partners and employees. During matches, there was always an extraordinary level of activity in the stadium, lots of partying, which created great energy between the people we brought. It was hard not to conclude that our experiences in the stadium helped create bonds between the people we brought in ways that made them a much stronger team afterward—both as friends and professionally.

In 2006, we gathered our sales reps from Germany in a big corporate box for one of Brøndby IF's matches, and after the match, most of them had become interested in the club. In this way, more and more exciting energy was generated around our Brøndby IF game activities that we organized. In Germany, they have a tradition for having some of their major clubs being so-called "workers' clubs." These clubs are supported by the local workers and businesses. Because Brøndby IF also has a tradition for this kind of support, we could see how our support for the team created a lot of sympathy in the eyes of our German business partners, customers, and employees. In other words, Brøndby IF was precisely what we needed to strengthen and develop a profile for KASI Group and our family—this kind of club association was something the Germans could totally identify with. We gradually upgraded our sponsorships, and at one point, we had reached a level where we had our own permanent sky box where we would eat and party with our customers and employees while also having a fantastic view of the entire stadium during the matches.

Then, in 2007, we had our really big breakthrough with respect to selling Pandora jewelry. The success was intoxicating, and for the first time I also realized how risky it could be. As our earnings went through the roof, we needed our corporate structure to match that development. And this meant that we desperately needed more German-speaking employees for our offices in Denmark. But when we advertised vacancies, we had no real takers. The problem was that we were physically located in Denmark, but our business was in Germany. We were trying to compete for the really good candidates against more visible companies. For example, when we posted a vacancy for a major position, such as a director of sales, we might only get a single paltry application from the manager of a local co-op who had never heard of us. One way to solve that problem was to move the entire company to Germany. But since my mom and sister were key employees in the organization and did not want to move, that option was not feasible.

One day my mom called me to tell me that Brøndby IF had lost its main sponsor. If our company could raise the almost $27 million necessary to become the new main sponsor, we would—due to Brøndby IF's status—become incredibly visible in the business community connected with the club. Without doubt, this would make us nationally known *and* solve our recruiting dilemma. Brøndby IF, at that point, was absolutely Denmark's strongest sports brand, so there were several bidders. But after a few discussions with Brøndby IF's management team, I managed to convince them that KASI Group had what it took. This meant that we were soon sitting alongside Brøndby IF's management to work out the final details of a future sponsorship agreement.

When KASI Group was announced as Brøndby IF's new main sponsor to the public, it worked like the ultimate quick fix. Overnight, I went from being an anonymous jewelry seller to a nationally known person. I was the mysterious businessman who had come from nowhere to become the main sponsor of Brøndby IF. Soon after, applications were pouring in from applicants—this time cream-of-the-crop candidates—several of whom would later help propel Pandora all the way to top of the international business scene. In tandem with this and because of the sponsorship, there was a new optimism in Brøndby IF. Still, they never quite reached the level I wanted them to. The year after I became their sponsor, they only won bronze in the Danish national soccer cup. It was a result that was clearly due to their poor and not particularly visionary leadership team. They simply made too many mistakes and misjudgments. At that time, I had been visiting German soccer clubs to see how they managed things. There was no doubt that the clubs there were light-years ahead of what Brøndby IF was capable of, and it became very clear to me that what Brøndby IF needed was a thorough cleanup—both in terms of the sports and commercial aspects. However, as a sponsor I had no influence on Brøndby IF's actions and when, after a few years, I decided to pull out as a sponsor, I had personally witnessed how a management team with no vision can lay waste to an otherwise excellent team's opportunity to reach the top.

My experiences of, literally, sitting on the sideline as a passive sponsor further fueled a question I had asked myself many times: What would happen if I took a completely obscure sports club that had never accomplished anything special and gave it some tender care and a vision? Could I use the knowledge I had gained from my work with Pandora to create a sports team that would become a world champion? My first thoughts about leading a small, invisible club to a world championship had already been hatched a few years earlier in discussions with my sister, Annette. At that time, we had not yet become main sponsors of Brøndby IF and were still experiencing enormous problems getting enough qualified employees for our business. On the plane back from a business meeting, Annette and I were discussing the problem, and my proposal was to perhaps become even more active in our work surrounding our local handball club. We might even use the club as a platform to recruit more employees. My sister thought it sounded like a grand idea, and as soon as we got back I contacted the club's chairman and requested a meeting.

Naturally, the chairman knew who I was. It was because of this club I became involved in handball—I had been an avid player since I was about eight years old. Later, I played on the club's premier team from the time I was 17 years old until I was 34. I still hold the record for the most premier team matches played. My dad has been in the club his entire life; my kids have played in the club; and my sister played there from the time she was a kid until she was 25 years old. I did not have the talent to become a professional, but I was at least as committed to the sport as many professionals are. Precisely because I did not move up to become a professional, I was surrounded by many of the same players throughout all the years I played. This meant that most of my close friends and almost all of my pals from my home town had some relationship or other with the club. Apart from my work, handball had always been the thing that was most significant in my life and something that, for many years, took up as much space as my work.

Everyone in the club knew us and knew that we had a company, but no one had any idea of the huge sums of money the company was making. A few days later the chairman came to visit, accompanied by two of my old handball teammates who were doing voluntary chores around the club. At the meeting I told them that our family had decided that we wanted to support the club with a tidy amount of money and that we believed that the club could be a good recruitment tool to find employees for our company in the future. As the meeting ended, I asked them to put their thinking caps on and draw up a proposal to how we might partner. I specifically pointed out that I was not looking for a regular draft proposal. We were looking at being *really* good so, please, submit a *really* ambitious discussion draft. They asked what exactly I meant by "ambitious," to which I replied that I had a vision of putting together the world's best handball team.

At this point, I should probably mention that the club was in what is called Series 1; in other words, it was ranked among the absolute bottom teams. It was a club you would only know of if you happened to play there, lived in the area, or spotted the street sign. In short, the distance to the stars was inconceivable to them. And since the chairman and the two volunteers had no idea that our company had that the kind of financial heft that it did, they must have left that meeting deeply puzzled. Here, they had taken this meeting with this person—their pal throughout many years—who had played on the club's premier team for an eternity without moving up, and here he was deliriously babbling on about putting together the world's best team. In spite of this, they nevertheless got back to me a couple of weeks later proposing developing a women's team. I rejected that straight away. The thing was that women's handball at the time of the meeting was doing quite well. But I had the sense that things would change in the near future, and there would be more focus on men's handball. If my sense was correct, we would be able to attract a lot of attention around the team and get the right kind of fan and sponsor attendance to eventually make our team a good business. I asked them to go back and give it some more thought, but this time with men's handball. At the time, this was naturally only a gamble on my part—but the chairman was open and went home, prepared a new proposal on men's handball, and soon we were ready to get going.

As mentioned, the team we were going to partner with was at the very bottom of the Danish handball league table hierarchy. If we were going to be the world champions, we would need to move up five divisions before we would even be allowed to play for the Danish championship. At the most, a club can only move up one division per year—and only if it does *really* well. Only if we became Danish champions would we be able to qualify to play internationally in the Champions League. From there, if all went well, you would move on to what was the absolute pinnacle: the Champions League Final Four. This is the final tournament where the four best clubs in Europe meet. Since almost all the good handball clubs are in Europe, the Final Four is often referred to as the world championship for club teams. This meant that, if we managed to go all the way without losing a tournament, we would have a shot at becoming the world's best handball team in six years. Naturally, to start out with a vision like that for an obscure club was completely absurd, but no matter. The strategy was to let the club grow slowly and, from year to year, attract new strong players who could bring the club the necessary steps up the ladder toward our goal.

Paradoxically, our first promotion was one of the most difficult we encountered. At the Series 1 level, players are not professional players, and it was difficult to attract new players to our club. The fact that they were associated with a certain club often had to do with their links to a particular club's network or its local community. In order to solve that challenge, I needed some help. One of my really good friends, Emeka Andersen, came to the rescue. Earlier in life, we had played handball together for many years, and now he joined us and was charged with ensuring our first promotion. Back when Emeka and I played handball, I was the playmaker, and he played left back. My task was to put together small systems and play him up so that he could break through the defense and score. We would team up constantly, and as I used to say: He was the brawn and I was the brains of that particular operation. Before Emeka started on this new outrageously ambitious project, he told me that I, regrettably, had become too old and creaky to be on the court. I may not have qualified to play on the team, but he believed he could still be useful in that capacity; but only for the first promotion. After that, we would need players better than him—but we could cross that bridge when we got to it.

The fact that it was Emeka who started things up meant that, from the very start, we managed to establish what was later to become such an important part of the team's DNA: his extreme will and capacity for winning. Not only does he *hate* to lose, he hates losing so much that training with him can be incredibly uncomfortable. During the years we trained together, I almost always tried to keep a healthy distance from him. To him, whether we were training or competing in a match was *completely* irrelevant. He would use any and all means to win, and even if you were best pals off the court you had better not get in his way. In many ways, Emeka is a fascinating guy. In his daily work, he deals with mentally retarded children and when he is not doing sports, he is calm, understanding, empathetic, and unexcitable. But, holy cow, once he crosses the chalked lines of a soccer pitch or enters an arena, he will kill to win. At the same time, he is incredibly adaptable and is colossally talented sports-wise. He was the goalie for Brøndby IF's super liga team, he holds an A license in boxing, he has been on the Danish bobsled team, has played American football, and has played handball at a relatively high level. Back when he and I played on the same team, we would sometimes warm up by playing basketball before moving on to handball. And let me tell you, with his 6'4", 220 lbs. frame he was not an easy opponent. Regardless of where you would hide on the court, when this pack of muscles came flying, bulldozing everyone, you had better get out of the way. Already from the start, he imprinted his particular mentality on our new men's team and actually remained on the team as an active player for no fewer than three divisional promotions—an incredible feat. After that, he transitioned into becoming the team's sports manager.

During the initial phase, it was Emeka who ran a great deal of the training; my role was to plan which players we would need from season to season. Of course, these would have to be players who could represent a team that would have the ability to advance, and this was often quite a difficult puzzle to solve. As our team, AGK, advanced year after year, I gradually gained more and more knowledge about how to grow a handball team. And it certainly helped and created a kind of symbiotic relationship that I had also become the owner of the German handball club, Rhein-Neckar Löwen, which in certain ways resembled AGK. For this period of three years, I was both owner and president of the Danish and German clubs, and I soaked up all the knowledge I could about how the world of handball works at the highest international levels. For example, it quickly became pretty clear to me that you cannot buy your way to success by assembling an "ultimate team." Even if you had the power, money, and wherewithal to buy up all the best players in the world, it would still be pretty doubtful that your team would actually prevail. The team might look fantastic on paper, but sports teams—and corporations—are complex organisms, and there are an incredible number of details that need to come together at the right time. Success is not only about individual players' performance. Your players need to be great individually, but they also need to be able to work as a team, to be able to sense where they have each other, and be comfortable with each other, etc. The knowledge I gradually acquired through my business activities, I transferred to my work with AGK. With that, we worked out a number of strategies as if it had been a straight down-the-line business—strategies that allowed for maximum levels of flexibility.

One of the aspects I paid particular attention to was to scout for the right players—and there was naturally a huge gap between the players I wanted and the ones I could have. In my efforts to find the right players, I tried to maintain a core of Danish players. The way I saw it, having too many non-Danish players might blur the team's profile. If we developed a Danish core, we could more easily create a home crowd of Danish fans, sponsors, and other stakeholders. Over the course of 2010, I managed to put together the ultimate team with major profiles who had previously played abroad and who actually should still be playing in Spain and Germany. Now they were suddenly gathered on a Danish team and that worked wonders—both for the team and for team support.

Another thing that influenced the way I put together the team was based on the special pleasure I took in seeing Icelandic players play. Iceland may be a tiny country, but they create completely unique handball players who rank among the very top in the world. Of course, the Icelandic players I included on our team did nothing to improve our Danish profile, but what they lacked in Danishness they made up in spades in winning mentality and their exceptional ability to generate energy on the team. As I was putting together the team to lead AGK, the last piece of the way to become world champions, nearly all handball experts made pronouncements on how silly and unrealistic my vision was and that many of my players were too old. Many people believe that older players cannot keep up physically. In truth, it is not so much their physical component that is weakened, but their motivation. From my work with Pandora, I had seen what can happen when you drag a person out into the sunlight who thought that he or she had reached the end of his career. If you give that person the motivation and the energy, he or she can accomplish things that no one had thought possible. At the same time, I also knew from my work at KASI Group that there was no use trying to base the world's best team on young stars alone. If a company or a team needs to develop properly, you need to make room for life experience. Several of the players we acquired grew dramatically while they played for the team. For example, the Danish star player, Mikkel Hansen, was named the world's best handball player while playing for us. There is not a doubt in my mind that our club and unique mentality had contributed to his incredible trajectory.

While working with the team, it was important to keep refining the framework for the players. Apart from getting the world's best trainers, they were also given access to the absolute proper diet, to the best sports therapists, and everything else imaginable that would allow them to function optimally. My approach was the same as the one I had used for the team that sold Pandora jewelry—and that is to eliminate any and all possible excuses for not being the world's best. By constantly creating the optimal framework, they had to succeed, they had to win every *single* time, and always do so with as many goals as possible.

The next step in taking the team to the very top had to do with creating exciting and different events for the matches. Through my work with Pandora, I had done road shows, and I decided to use that same approach to make AGK a crowd puller. If you do not know handball and the story around the sport, I should mention that while we were developing AGK, there was no tradition for handball being an event. Previously, for many years, you might say that the people who turned up for games were a small core of diehard former-player devotees. The question was whether or not we could find a greater and wider audience that would not only be excited by handball as a sport but also handball as an event. If we could get regular people with children to buy tickets to watch handball, it would have a favorable impact on our finances and on the number of fans as well as the interest from our sponsors. Therefore, the matches—as we see in basketball, ice hockey, soccer, football, and baseball—had to be transformed into events, which would make the sport more palatable to a broader audience. I therefore decided to invest lots of time and money into making matches into a kind of *total theater* events that would give our audience a completely unique participatory experience. The goal was to have spectators leave matches completely overwhelmed, not just from the match itself but also from the show they had just witnessed. It was primarily my sister and I who pulled the heavy load of orchestrating and executing the events for the matches, but I was naturally assisted by the best people in that field. As I saw it, it was about using all the means at our disposal to touch our audience as much as possible emotionally. I used to characterize what we were creating as "emotional immersion"—it needed to give you goose bumps. And as far as giving people that sensation, I was quite detail oriented. To create those goose bump experiences, we had various tools at our disposal the most important of which, without doubt, was the music. As a young boy, of course, I had been an enthusiastic amateur DJ. It was an interest that had taught me a lot about how music can give people a sense of unity and open them up emotionally. For my work with the game events, I allied myself with a guy who was known for being the best sports DJ in Europe. To get our spectators on their feet, we needed fanfares and applause jingles they could relate to. I spent a great deal of money to have a composer write various songs that paid tribute to our team in various ways.

Actually, the events surrounding the handball matches represented 90 percent of the work involved in playing matches at home. These had to be managed like clockwork and be executed in ways that would give our audience an unforgettable experience, while also involving them actively during the event. We would start the music two hours before the actual match by setting up a whole little universe for kids, which we called the Fun Zone. There, the kids could run around and play handball, complete a dribble track and get scorecards. And, if they did well, they would win little trophies and candy. They could also measure how hard they could throw: "Mikkel Hansen can throw the ball 82 mph— what's your speed?" Of course, our Fun Zone was a way to get young people interested in the game that we ourselves loved so much while also showing them that exercise can be fun. But it also turned out to be a fantastic way to get young people to the arena well ahead of the game. And, as our audience gradually realized that we did this, many would start lining up at the gates two hours before the match even started. One hour before the match, we would pack away the Fun Zone and the players would get on the court to warm up. This happened 45 minutes before the match started, and the fans were already in their seats looking forward to the match. While the players warmed up, we would have a professional stadium announcer on the court presenting the players one by one. This helped to build up the players by giving them a proper introduction. I should also point out that the order in which they were introduced was carefully chosen. Naturally, it was important to have the last player entering the court to warm up also be the biggest star, and when that finally happened, the whole stadium was completely euphoric. During the warm-up the players were also filmed individually and shown on a jumbotron as they were presented one-by-one. The player's individual melody would be played, as well as the little music snippet that would be played when he scored. For example, when the goalie did a save, a snippet would be played from Tina Turner's "Simply The Best." When Mikkel Hansen would score, we would play a snippet from MC Hammer's "U Can't Touch This!" Or, when our defensive giant, Lars Jørgensen, would get into the scoring zone, we would play AC/DC's "TNT." Both the players and the audience soon learned all the tunes by heart and went completely crazy when they were played.

The next part of the event was playing the AGK anthem, and that happened precisely 17 minutes and 52 seconds before the match started. Once the players had left the court, our singer was ready to sing our tribute to the best handball team in the world while we had everyone in the stadium sing along, clap, and cheer. After the song, it was time for the fanfare which, in my eyes, was the most unadulterated emotional and goose bump–inducing event. For this part of the program, we would turn off the lights and have four huge banners moving around the entire stadium only lit by a softened stroboscope spotlight. Then it was time to present the referees, the match and ball sponsors of the day, but also our court assistant boys, the small boys from the neighborhood who would run in to dry up the water or sweat from the court. Before the next item, which was the highlight of the day, we needed to sneak our opponents onto the court—this was a pretty quiet affair, which more or less took place in darkness. And then! In an absolute inferno of light, lasers, smoke, and sound, our boys entered the court. Again, here we had a regular song, which was a rewrite of an old Pet Shop Boys song that would be sung in a full-throated rendition by the entire stadium. During this song, the players would enter the court as if shot from a cannon. Each time the expectant spectators let out a deafening roar. For the match itself, we would continue our work with the various show business components we had perfected. For instance, if we were ahead by five goals we would play our five-goal jingle and caramels would be showered out onto the audience. In developing the event, we also introduced a partnership with McDonald's, which would sell Big Macs at half-price for the rest of the evening in all their many Copenhagen restaurants if we managed to get ahead by ten goals. Simultaneously, throughout the entire match, our DJ would celebrate each goal or play music each time our team was on the offensive so that people would immediately be on their feet cheering on our team. This method of generating energy around matches was the most important component in building up events—each event would be bigger than the previous event. I have personally attended an incredible number of sports events—I am not afraid to admit that I am like a sponge. I take all the best stuff I see, tweak it, and incorporate it into my own events. For example, instead of regular cheerleaders, I would use what we called a Sports Team Playitas, which was a gymnastics team that would enter the court and perform or initiate applause as soon as there was a timeout. Then, at halftime, we would always have various major bands perform. Everything we added to the match created an incredibly heated atmosphere in the stadium which not only meant that our audience was happy and—in something that is unheard of for handball—that *all* of our games were always sold out.

The objective of building up events around a match as total theater was to create a fan culture that could help strengthen and build up many different facets of the club. As one might expect, our approach also created its share of animosity from our opponents who thought we were psyching them out before and during the matches. But it was hard to argue that we did not achieve exceptional results: Our team never lost a home match. Also, there were many negative voices among the people who came from the established handball world; they did not like the change for which we had suddenly become exponents. I have to say that it did not bother me one bit. On the contrary, it was exciting to see how much we were able to revolutionize and re-energize the entire environment and culture surrounding handball. Our showmanship not only helped our players on home court, but it also helped draw in kids and young players by making it glamorous. Another and equally important factor was that we wanted to influence our sponsors. As our sponsors took their seats in the VIP section, it was impossible for them to not feel the infectious energy of the total theater we had created. From my time as a sponsor in Brøndby IF, I knew how important it was when the sponsors were caught up in the excitement and energy, which in turn prompted them to commit themselves further to the club. I know from my own experience as a sponsor that one of the most important things for sponsors is that their experience should be one they want to share with their customers or business partners. And, we could tell from how things developed, that a lot of sponsors wanted that experience.

To the great disappointment of many critics, our team advanced five years in a row, and we reached the Handball League in 2010 having won all the tournaments and competitions we participated in. In 2011, as we were about to play for gold in Denmark, I decided that this was the right time to show Denmark just how big handball could become. I decided to rent the Danish national soccer stadium, Parken, for the final playoffs. My plan was to fill it to capacity with 36,000 spectators. If we could do that, we would set a new world record for the biggest audience for a handball match ever. Naturally, I saw this as one of my big stunts. I wanted to show my business partners and employees the potential of handball. We had the right team, the right setup, and we had everything in place to create the ultimate event. At the same time, it was also a bit of a gamble. If I did this and only 10,000 spectators showed up, frankly I would look like a bit of a jerk who had bitten more off than he could chew. The question was how I could be sure that I would be able to create the kind of success I was looking for. Many others would probably start drawing up studies to evaluate whether or not an audience would be attracted to such an event. What I did was to sleep on it, and when I woke up in the morning I checked to see what my gut feeling would be. That feeling was a clear "yes"—of course it could be done! I then gathered my employees and told each of them individually that they needed to do their utmost on this one. We only had three weeks to prepare and to sell all the tickets, and before that, our team would be playing an away game. If they lost that game and won at home, there would have to be another match. So I took a giant gamble and told myself that we would win that away game and that our team would be able to celebrate their national championship after the national stadium match. When we announced my vision of doing the world's biggest handball match, there were many who were sure that I had finally gone completely over the edge. I took this as a challenge, and my colleagues and I got started. What made things happen was the hype that was created when people around the country started having this urge to be present at what would be the world's biggest handball match. This was not 36,000 people who only came to see handball. It was 36,000 people coming to witness a unique event.

Fortunately, and to my great relief, things went just the way I had predicted. For the first match away, AGK won by two goals. So, 36,000 people streamed into the Danish national stadium in 2011 where they witnessed AGK bringing home the gold and becoming Danish champions by a spectacular score of 30-21. After this extraordinary feat, I did not go out on the town with the players and all our ecstatic fans and supporters. No, I spent that evening with Emeka. This was a complete dream, and it had started with him and his fanatical drive to win. So, it only felt right that it would be he and I spending this special evening celebrating in each others' company.

With the national championship behind us, the next step was the Champions League, which could lead us to the European Championship in the following year—an accomplishment that would effectively make us world champions. As something very atypical for a sports team, we reached all the targets we had set for ourselves leading up to the Champions League. It was a great source of satisfaction to me to be able to look back at my six years with the team without having been disappointed in their performance and accomplishments even once. To me, personally, there was of course an element of personal satisfaction with respect to my sponsorship experiences with Brøndby IF: I finally had a sports team that was totally superior and fully met all of my demands for a supreme performance. During this long journey with AGK, there were many highlights. One that stands out took place in 2012. We met Barcelona, which had won the Champions League the year before and which bore the title of the best handball team in the world. This match, too, had been arranged to take place at the national stadium before 21,300 spectators. In the audience, there were 3,000 VIP guests, and the match was watched in 61 countries by 131 million viewers. The previous year we had set a record with the biggest audience at a handball match ever, but this time we set the record with the most spectators for a Champions League match ever. Even though Barcelona was far from the easiest opponent we could have drawn, we nevertheless decided to go into it with a positive spirit. The match also promised to become a great business success, and it certainly fulfilled that promise. Tickets for the match were sold for about $70 a piece, and because we had no problems selling all the seats, we ended up with a nice profit on the tickets alone. It was, of course, also a unique international event which made our fan base go through the roof. Apart from this, we were now also so big that it was not only our fans who poured in but also our sponsors. Finally, we had 480 companies as sponsors at a total value of nearly $13.5 million, and when we finally ran at full speed, we managed to get 40 to 50 new sponsors into the fold per month. Following the match against Barcelona, the news agencies published the following text:

"On Friday night in front of a record backdrop, AGK won 29-23 over defending European Champions, Barcelona. Following an outstanding effort, the Danish champions showed us that they truly belong among Europe's best teams. The only question is whether the victory is big enough when the Danes go to Barcelona next Saturday. However, with this performance, AGK has given itself an excellent opportunity to become one of the four best teams in Europe."

As history shows, we then went to Spain and lost by three goals to Barcelona. During the long journey of growth with AGK, the team had played hundreds of matches with changing players and had only suffered seven defeats but had never lost by more than three goals. This time we had lost against Barcelona at an away game, but because we had won by six goals on our home court, we advanced. We had reached the Final Four tournament, the final step in our dream, to be played in an arena in Cologne, Germany, before 20,000 spectators. The year before, I had already been there with my German handball club, where we had also managed to qualify for the tournament. That meant that I was there for the second year in a row and had some experience with the environment there. In the semifinals, we met Atlético Madrid and finished the first half with a lead of five goals. When I met the players in the locker room, the mood was great and everyone agreed that this match was ours for the taking. It may have looked promising, but we still failed to win. And once the match was over, we had lost by two goals.

Even though I was disappointed that our first showing in a tournament did not result in a win, I quickly let go of my frustration and realized that it was all right. If we had won that first year, it might have come too soon, too fast— it was fine that we now had a little more time to build up things more solidly. Denmark had never previously had a team in the Final Four. That, in itself, was a fantastic accomplishment. That we had advanced as fast and as far as we did was almost beyond comprehension. Before we returned home, we won solidly over Berlin with six goals, and we traveled back to Denmark with a bronze medal. In other words, in 2012 we ended up being the third best team in the world—it was not the absolute pinnacle but not at all shabby. As soon as we were back in Copenhagen, we immediately started our preparations to return in 2013, to haul in the victory that had been my vision all along. We started out by recruiting the winning team's top player, and people generally started to view us as favorites for the world's top team slot in 2013.

Stunt No. 8

The positive mistakes

On standing by your mistakes and on using them constructively

There is hardly anything more human that our capacity to err. Lots of people are afraid of making mistakes and are constantly trying to avoid them. And when people do make mistakes, they are afraid to accept responsibility for them. Throughout my career I have regularly made mistakes, and they have often created special problems for me and others. But since making mistakes is a natural human thing, they are not something I will try to hide. If I have an employee who has made a mistake, I would never dream of getting upset or angry or rebuke or berate him or her. As mentioned, since I believe in the best in everyone, I know that the person in question will have done everything in his or her power to achieve the best possible result. If a mistake happens, the last thing we need is to introduce an element of guilt.

Before I started KASI, I had the world's easiest jobs. In these places, they had employee handbooks and if anyone asked you about something, you could just say: "Oh, wait, hang on! I just need to look up the answer to that in our employee handbook." The problem with employee handbooks is that by writing them, you are basing your business on rules that emasculate your organization completely. Many years ago, I therefore decided to do away with employee handbooks altogether. If we do not have a book like that, I cannot blame my employees when they make wrong decisions. As long as there is no employee handbook with rules for what is right and wrong, you are forced to think for yourself at all times. This way I force my entire organization to apply the principle I believe is the most important organizational principle in any business—to use your common sense. So each time one of my managers is in a difficult situation, he or she is forced to ask: "What do I think is the right thing to do right now?" In this way, you transfer a lot of expertise and growth from a central management team into the field. Throughout my entire career, I have been extremely reluctant to overrule any of my managers who have decided to make their own decision. Perhaps I will sit down with the person in question and perhaps give him or her a different perspective on the decision that was taken. If a decision needs to be remade, I will not do it since it would immediately undermine the manager and the decision he had already made.

If you can work with that kind of philosophy in place, you create a great sense of security for your employees, because they will always know where they have you. As an example of this, at one point I had a very senior executive in my organization who held a Christmas lunch for his employees. After the Christmas lunch, they ended up in a club that was on the exclusive end of the price scale. It was one of those places where any employee with a sound mind would have known that that is not the place to spend your company's money. In his intoxication, the executive in question nonetheless managed to use his company card to pick up the bar tab, spending close to $9,500 throughout the evening. Even though he knew that I put great stock in having fun, no one in the organization had any doubt that you can not just throw away the company's money like that. The following day the executive in question came into my office to tell me how incredibly sorry he was and that he was quite aware that he had done something wrong. In the kinds of situations where I am face to face with an employee who knows that he or she has done something wrong, I will give him as much of a safety net as I can. I just told him that it was probably not that bad, and that—with all the effort he had put into the business—I would be quite happy to give him a bit of leeway. It is all about being quick to put out the safety net as soon as he feels he is on shaky ground. In that situation it was pretty important for him to feel that I was not only there for him when he was successful, but also when he had forgotten to use his common sense. When this kind of discussion is over, it is important for it to be definitively over so that the person who claimed responsibility for the mistake does not need to worry that I will get back to him at some later stage to confront him with what he once did.

With time, I have actually even started seeing it as a great growth opportunity for the company when employees make mistakes. What started as a mistake will perhaps turn into the most brilliant thing we have ever done. When you have employees who are not afraid of trying things and go in new directions, you also discover paths that the competitors would never dare travel. Sure, mistakes are sometimes made, but the individual employee must be permitted to try out both his or her own and the company's boundaries, because this creates growth and mobility within the organization. If the person has a leader willing to lend support and who will continue to back him or her up 100 percent no matter what, that person is free to make his or her own mark on the organization. In all the time I have run a business, I have never gotten rid of an employee because of what you might, to borrow a term from tennis, call a foot fault—that is, a situation where you make a procedural error or the error of violating a set of rules.

In many organizations, they use a lot of energy chasing foot faults down to the very smallest details. In the general public, it is seen as an exciting and important game to bust some senior person for having submitted the wrong voucher. That is never my way. For example, if one of my executives had fueled his car by using his company card by mistake, you could say that was a foot fault. But in reality it has nothing to do with whether or not he will be able to function in his or her job. I do not really focus my efforts on that kind of stuff, and I will constantly try to get that executive person to sense what is right and what is wrong for himself. For executives that have been under me for years, they have always been very fascinated by this approach to management. For example, it would never occur to me to access their electronic calendar systems to see what they have scheduled for when. In fact, I have no idea where they are, what they are doing when, and whom they are with. The only thing I insist on, and that is a rule that we *never* deviate from, is that if I call them for a meeting, they *must* attend. Since it happens so rarely, there are absolutely no acceptable excuses, and a cancellation will be viewed in the most negative terms. Even if it is a board meeting at 11:30 p.m. in Mallorca, everyone must be there. If they fail to show up, this is the only error you risk being reprimanded for if you work for me.

Stunt No. 9

Relations

On private space and the so-called "whole leader"

Many people experience having problems with their families in their lives—they rebel against their parents or lose touch with their siblings when they move away from home. I am fully aware of how unusual it is that my sister and I have always been able to get along so well with our parents. If one of us has a problem, it is a problem for all four of us. If one of us is facing a difficult challenge, the other three will be sympathetic and will be good at providing support. Whatever we have, we share and whenever something needs to be done, we are always doing it together. At the same time, we are very different and therefore complement each other in every way. This is the most important reason my mom and sister have functioned as my closest business partners over the past many years. All these years, the roles we have assumed have felt completely natural. I am the younger brother and in public I take up the entire picture. However, inside my family things look completely different. Our close family relationship, which has allowed us to work so well together, has never been unhappy, and there has never been a feeling that my mom took up too much space or tried to take over in places where she should have stayed in the background. My sister does not have my wildness and capacity to be visionary, but she has a degree in law and is extremely competent. When she works on a project, everything is always 100% in order. In terms of our profiles, I would say that my mom and I bear a closer resemblance than my sister and I. Before my mom assumed a central role in KASI, she had a completely normal job for many years. Privately, throughout my entire childhood, she managed the home with a firm hand. My dad took care of his job and when he came home from work, everything was under control. My mom is what I would call a bull terrier; once she gets hold of something, she refuses to let go, and she works with an intensity that sometimes seems insane. A while back, our headquarters had a staff of 120; my mom managed it all with a firm yet loving hand. When she finally retired from that position because she needed to work less, I actually had to hire three men to fill her shoes.

I never had any need to be in opposition or rebel against my parents. Throughout my entire life, there has not been a single time when my parents did not stand behind me—regardless of what I had done. Therefore, I can easily say that my dad is the nicest human being I have ever met in my life. As a person, he is so friendly and helpful that he is completely beyond any category of any person I have ever met. My dad has always been an incredibly hard worker and has never had any use for complaining if something went against him. I simply do not believe you would find a single person on this planet who would have anything bad to say about him. He is just the way he is. He has also had the effect that my children often feel more connected to their granddad than to me. Because of my visions and eagerness to create something out in the world, I have often been away on business. But my dad is the person who compensates when I travel like I do. Regardless of what the kids need, he will be there, and he is always open and positive with them. In other words, you might say that the "yes philosophy" I have practiced in my business vis-à-vis my customers is the philosophy that my dad is practicing in relation to my family and our friends.

In business there is a lot of talk about what they call the "whole leader." As I understand it, it is about being whole and seeking to make distinctions between your work life and your family life. To me it is completely absurd to even contemplate that kind of distinction. There has always been a natural link between what happened in our family and what happened in my work life. These two parts of my life have always been linked and acted as catalysts for each other. This is perhaps the reason I have always felt it was a strength when the people I was working closely with also began to come to my private home or me to theirs. It is in the private sphere that you feel who you really are in relation to each other and where you can create an experience that both parties are pretty ordinary people—even if, outside the home, you have been able to create quite extraordinary things. One's private life is the best place to meet if you want to eliminate stuff that is fake or pretentious.

Life Story Part 3

The takeover

On letting go of your most cherished possession

To understand the background for what else happened with AGK and what would probably qualify as one of the world's most improbable and extraordinary sports adventures, I need to rewind a bit and look at some of the business decisions I made in 2008. This was the year when something happened that I had feared for so many years. The old owners of Pandora decided to sell their business. They did so to the private equity fund, Axcel. Even though my company also distributed products from suppliers other than Pandora, about 90 percent of our earnings came from Pandora jewelry. The relatively small share of earnings from other products meant that we were overexposed and extra vulnerable to Pandora. At any time they could decide to pull the plug and not renew our contract to distribute their products. Needless to say, this would cause serious problems for our company. The new equity, fund-backed management team who took over at Pandora, guided by strict logic and a rational, traditional management style, quickly noticed that I was earning huge sums of money as the exclusive dealer in the markets Pandora had allocated to me. They quickly started asking questions along the lines of why they could not just chuck us out and earn that money for themselves. After all, I had already done the heavy lifting of fertilizing and cultivating the entire Pandora ecosystem. So, what was to stop them from letting us simply wither on the vine by letting my contract expire and then just taking over everything? The old management team had an ethics code—this was something that would never have occurred to them. The new management team had a different kind of approach to things: We would no longer be doing business built on friendship, ethics, and compassion. Instead, we would now be doing business based on ice-cold data. Of course, the new Pandora was in a very strong position in relation to me. At any point, they would be able to make me skip, jump, and dance to their tune whenever they felt like it—and they started to feel like it quite quickly.

They drafted a plan to take over my business but were reasonably careful not to flush the enormous success I had created out with the bathwater. If they had just let my contract expire, they would not necessarily have been able to gain access to the infrastructure I had built up with my suppliers, sales representatives and with my customers, and the good will that had been created around Pandora. At the time, they were also aware that I was very visible in the German jewelry market, and I had built up our success by establishing personal relationships with all my customers. If the new management team were to decide to get rid of me, it might very well also mean that the customers I had created would get rid of Pandora altogether.

In 2009, I therefore received an "offer" that—as the phrase goes—I could not refuse. If I said no, they would let my contract expire; if I said yes, I needed to cooperate and quite "voluntarily" hand over my life's work and all my employees to Pandora. If I agreed to the arrangement, I would get $81 million in my hand as well as a share of Pandora's profits for the next five fiscal years while also serving as the CEO of the new company. According to the offer, I would continue to grow our success while Pandora would gradually take over my business. Therefore, in the following period, all KASI Group activities would be wound down and the company put on ice. After that, a new company would be established under the big global Pandora A/S, which was named "Pandora Central Western Europe" or Pandora CWE. This was the company in which I would serve as CEO. Since KASI Group was shut down, there was no longer any point to maintaining my sponsorship of the soccer club, Brøndby IF. In that same year I decided to pull out and had to pay a penalty of $27 million to Brøndby IF, at which point the club was free to find a different main sponsor.

Many people have subsequently wondered why I did not like the contract I was given when Pandora CWE took over my life's work. Here we were, my family and I, being given a golden egg—we were financially secure for the rest of our lives. The problem is, and many people do not understand this, that the organization I had created from scratch represented something that was worth far more to me than just money. Let me put it in a different way: If one day you were forced to sell one of your children for a fortune, and this meant that you would be financially secure ever after, would you do it? When, as an entrepreneur and hardcore enthusiast, you create something like I had created, it naturally becomes the apple of your eye, and there is no amount of money that can compensate for the kind of loss I felt having to let go of that business. So, I stood there with a very big check in my hand but feeling that my KASI ship had been taken over by pirates who, bit by bit, were poaching my life's work.

Over the next four years I would not only be the entrepreneur who nourished the apple of his eye, but also a CEO under employment who, in actuality, was nothing but his executives' and the board's extended arm. Nevertheless, I started my time as CEO in my typical style. This meant that Pandora CWE continued to expand at lightning speed in Europe. However, it also became more and more obvious to me that the style the board of directors dictated to me was a style I had a very hard time identifying with. The primary problem was that almost none of the commands that were handed down from above had any chance of actually working in the organization I had created. The fact was that the new efficiency-minded management team at Pandora could not wrap their minds around how my business functioned. My entire infrastructure was anchored in personal relationships; it was about respect between people; about energy, closeness, and presence; and about the story you create around you when you show genuine interest in each other. What my colleagues and I sold to our customers was not just Pandora's jewelry, it was also joy, emotion, and social cohesion. A business school degree and spreadsheets and charts will not tell teach you this. With respect to the new board of directors, they spent all their time gathering figures from the various subsidiaries they had captured, and since those figures looked fantastic, the board figured they could walk on water. It was, in fact, a case of how quickly people can assume ownership of and take credit for a success they have had little part in creating. After the board of directors had been in office for only about three months, it managed to delude itself into thinking that its directors were the reason everything went so well. The board then made a great number of decisions without consulting those of us who actually had direct knowledge of our customers and the markets. No, this was an opportunity—or so they thought—to introduce new terms and conditions to our customers, a different approach to employees, new ways to draw up strategies and launch new collections. At the same time, I was supposed to serve as the messenger for a management team who clearly did not have the least grasp for the jewelry industry or the life's work I had created. With respect to our "cooperative arrangement," I was in total disagreement with nearly all the decisions handed down from the new CEO of Pandora A/S, who represented the global market. This applied to the products we were launching, to our approach to customers, and to the treatment of our employees. I tried to pull things in a direction that would fit the profiles of my employees and customers, only to be reprimanded from above. It is an understatement to say that I did not exactly thrive in this kind of environment.

Of the many hopeless decisions that issued from Pandora's new board of directors, one, in particular, outdid the rest of them in plain bone-headedness. According to this decision, Pandora's jewelry would transition from being a brand that could be purchased by regular people to becoming a luxury brand that would primarily be bought by the wealthiest people. If you can imagine a worldwide restaurant chain with enormous success making delicious and healthy quality food for regular people, it will give you some idea of how absurd it would be if it suddenly tried to transform itself into a chain of high-end expensive gourmet restaurants.

Pandora's management team decision would effectively leave a vacuum in the mainstream segment Pandora had established itself in and totally dominated. At the same time, it would lead Pandora into a segment where there was already fierce competition. Previously, we had been available to everyone; the new vision for the future laid waste to this ambition. The problem was clearly that our board knew nothing at all about our customers or about how business was transacted out in the field. None of them had worked their way up in the company and gained experience with the world we were dealing with on a day-to-day basis. They had taken over the entire company because they had money to spend and could tell that Pandora was a goldmine that could be mined for even more money. I can only guess at how the decision arose to cannibalize our core segment, but it was likely that the new top management were themselves among the wealthiest people and thought there might be more prestige in dealing in a luxury brand.

After the takeover, I fought the new management team tooth and claw, and because this was a business I had created myself, I probably did so for much longer than I should have done. The trouble was that this was my life's work, and because I had created every little niche in our fantastic organization, it was painful to see how it was being destroyed and neglected. In 2011, I finally came to terms with the fact that the battle was lost. If I continued, I could no longer look myself in the mirror, and I decided to pull out of Pandora CWE. After six years of spending all my energy on proselytizing a certain philosophy to my customers and colleagues, it had come to the point when the management team had started dictating that I needed to do exactly the opposite of everything I had ever talked about. It naturally seemed wildly frivolous, and it confused everyone who kept asking me what would happen next. During that period I daily heard the following question: "But Jesper! For several years, you have told us that we would do certain things. Now you are telling us to do exactly the opposite. I'm confused—what do you think we should do?"

I recently had lunch with one of my previous customers in Germany who told me that 18 months after I had stopped working for Pandora, he had still not met the person who took over after me at Pandora CWE. Naturally, my replacement was a man who fit right into the streamlined culture the top management team was looking to create, and he spent all of his time at his office with his nose buried in papers instead of traveling out to meet his customers. This new style created a backlash among the customers. From having a personal relationship with the person you are trading with, you are now interacting with sales machines. This was a shock to customers and resulted in a lot of poor publicity for Pandora. The customers' reactions to the new style were also quite clearly reflected in Pandora's financial statements. And briefly after pulling out, Pandora experienced—for the first time since I had started out—that its earnings stagnated. In addition to this, my break with the company also created a strong reaction among my former colleagues. To them, it was completely absurd that the person who had hired them and in whom they had complete trust was all of a sudden *persona non grata* in the new management team's eyes.

In 2012, I attended a jewelry trade show in Munich which featured, among other things, Pandora's products. Even though more than one year had elapsed since I had left the company, I was told that everyone at the trade show was talking about my arrival. In recent years, I had been such a central element to Pandora's marketing efforts that I had become one of the most well-known faces in the German jewelry industry. If you ask a German jeweler today what Pandora is, he will still say that Pandora is Jesper Nielsen.

During my visit to the trade show, I wanted to pay a quick visit to the booth that presented Pandora's products. But before I could get there, I was told to just stay away. Just think how easily the new management team could have turned around the resistance many of my former employees felt toward them after I had left the business. If the new management team would have just welcomed me in front of my former colleagues with a hug and a pat on the shoulder instead, they would have been able to score an enormous number of points both among their own employees and the customers. There is an old proverb that suggests that a well-placed bullet can change world history. The same principle might also apply to hugs.

At the time of the equity fund's takeover of my Pandora, the handball club flourished like never before. Instead of spending my energy on Pandora, I decided to focus my energy on the handball club which was riding a constant wave of success. But even though AGK lived up to my expectations in every way, there was still something that bothered me. As previously mentioned, in 2008 an employee had disclosed confidential materials to the press because he had not been invited to join the top management team of my company. After that, most of the tabloids had adopted a negative tone toward my activities. Everything I did was scrutinized in minute detail, and regardless of how well everything went, it seemed that all the stories would somehow be given a negative spin.

This development naturally had a very negative impact on our sponsors' confidence in AGK. I realized that unless the press would let go of me, it might have fatal consequences for my handball club. Over the summer of 2012, the press intensified their absurd campaign and started chasing me in a more and more targeted manner. During this period, the stories primarily dealt with the Danish tax authorities' interest in the sponsorship I had signed with Brøndby IF years back. I had paid the sponsorship from my company's advertising budget, but the tax authorities failed to see how a sponsorship could be a commercial transaction. Under Danish tax law, if you sponsor a sports club you must obtain corresponding advertisement for the purpose of achieving anticipated additional sales. If not, the sponsorship should be considered a gift payable from funds already taxed. The tax authorities saw my sponsorship as a gift since they were unable to determine how I had sold more jewelry in Denmark as a result of the sponsorship. At a meeting with the tax authorities, I explained that I had not taken out the sponsorship to sell jewelry in Denmark but to advertise my company for the purpose of recruiting employees and attracting collaborators and stakeholders. At the same time, my sponsorship had also resulted in the success my entire German sales network in Brøndby IF had achieved, and that the club had successfully advertised for my company when it played abroad. The sponsorship had therefore helped me sell more jewelry both at home and abroad. These arguments held no interest to the tax authorities at all, and after an unproductive dialog with them, I decided to just let my lawyer work out the details.

In the summer of 2012, I was sitting at my regular hangout at Mallorca having just finished lunch. I gave the waiter my credit card and was about to leave. The waiter knows me, and he apogized profusely when he returned my card. It was rejected. I quickly found a different credit card; that did not work either. I finally gave him my credit card from my German bank, and that worked. The situation rang an alarm bell in my subconscious, and I called home to talk to my sister briefly. Same story there: she had tried to withdraw money, but the ATM had rejected her card. I then contacted my mom, who told me that she had no idea what was going on—she would just peek to see if there was anything we might have overlooked in our mailbox. She quickly got back to me: There was a pile of mail from the enforcement court and the tax authorities who had contacted us through the Legal Advisor to the Danish Government. The message was that they had seized *all* of our assets. They had put a lien on my parents' cars, on our houses, on my kids' savings accounts and everywhere else they could. I later learned that the Legal Advisor to the Danish Government only decides to take such drastic steps if the person they are targeting is deeply involved in criminal activities. That they decided to take such draconian steps with me and my family—I later discovered—was a result of the negative press coverage. If I had been a regular businessman who had not had such a prominent profile in the media, they would have instead asked me to simply provide security for any potential judgment, if they were going to pursue legal action against me.

The following days I had no idea what the tax authorities and the Legal Advisor to the Danish Government were up to. The first time I saw in writing what the tax authorities believed I owed them was on the front page of a newspaper. It said, in large type, that I owed the tax authorities upward of $33.5 million. In the first place, it had not at all been established that I owed *any* money at all in taxes; in the second place, Danish law is quite specific that tax proceedings are not pursued in public—they are deeply private matters subject to strict disclosure laws. If you have an outstanding balance with the tax authorities, that is a private matter between you and them. Thankfully, it was not difficult to get the management of the tax authorities to see the problem, and the director of the Danish Ministry of Taxation decided to report the tax authorities to the police himself for violating their duty of confidentiality.

Still, the damage was done, and the public hanging that had been put into motion obliterated my business reputation. In addition, my family and especially my kids had to be confronted with reports that their dad was a criminal and was being presented to the general public as if I gone completely bust. While all this was going on, the Legal Advisor to the Danish Government had seized a major portion of my family's assets.

The result of what happened in the press was reflected quite clearly in AGK's development as a business. We went from getting 40 to 50 new sponsors a month before the hounding in the press, to none while it was going on. Since a great deal of my and my family's funds had been frozen by the Legal Advisor's office, we did not know whether or not we could find the money to run the club for the rest of the season. Therefore, we made a number of rapid and drastic decisions with respect to AGK. One of the things we agreed on in the family was that we had had enough of the treatment we had received in the public press. One of my intentions with AGK was that I, as a successful businessman, would return to my native town and give the community there some great experiences. It was all supposed to be fun and something we could all take joy in and be proud of. Instead, it had developed into my being pulled out for public humiliation and branded a criminal. The question to me was why I would want to let myself and my family be treated that way. Even though I had never thought I would arrive at that conclusion, I realized that there actually were, in fact, more important things in life than handball at the highest levels. The costs related to the whole circus that accompanied it were simply too high, both emotionally and in terms of business. During some hectic days, we tried various rescue actions. But as things stood, it was just too risky to carry on. On that basis, I had to make one of my life's most difficult decisions: to close the club and move on.

The outcome of this decision was naturally a great disappointment to all the people who had been looking forward to seeing if we could become the world's top handball team in 2013. Apart from that, it was a disappointment to all of AGK's employees, for its 530,000 supporters, and for our 480 sponsors. Soon after the doors were locked and the lights turned off, the players were spread out to other clubs and many of the people who were either supporters of the club or had had a successful partnership with the club either became disappointed or very angry at me and my family. It is hard to blame them, since almost no one outside our close circle knew the factual circumstances of the story.

In the weeks after I was forced to close AGK, something happened that made the tide turn with the general public. In the media, there were a number of embarrassing revelations regarding the tax authorities' methods, and the tax authorities' attacks on me gradually abated. After I was "allowed" to spend about $400,000 on drawing up cash flow analyses that showed that all my financial transactions had, in fact, been perfectly legal and on the up-and-up, they lifted the freezing of my funds and instead gave me the opportunity to provide guarantees. In this way, the tax authorities felt secure that they would get their money in case they were going to prevail in the eventuality they ever decided to pursue a case before the courts. In the media, the case surrounding the tax authorities continued to evolve, and the tax authorities soon tried several different rescue operations to rectify their very tarnished image in the general public's eyes. Suddenly, I received a letter with a 10-page long apology from the tax authorities in which they admitted that their treatment of me and my family had, in fact, been appalling. The letter stated that the individuals who had persecuted me had been suspended and that they had postponed my case indefinitely. That meant that a big part of my assets would remain untouched until such time as they decided to bring a case before a court of law. At this stage, they they were undoubtedly fully aware that they would lose the case, but there were likely people higher up in the food chain who preferred to prolong the matter as long as they could before their incompetence was exposed in the media.

If you are not Danish, and if you want to understand how my story could develop the way that it did, you need to understand a part of the Danish mentality that we locally refer to as the Law of Jante (otherwise known as the Law of Who-Do-You-Think-You-Are?). The Jante Law is of course not a law in the traditional sense; rather, it is part of a mentality that is widespread in all of Scandinavia, including Denmark. Briefly, it is about a fear of and aversion to people who believe in themselves and in their own abilities. According to this mindset, it is an offense to believe that you are special, that you are better than anyone else, that you are more important, or that you could possibly have anything others might be interested in. I may have my roots in a tiny country like Denmark where the Jante Law is so ingrained in everything, but there is really nothing more remote and alien to me. Today, I can see that it can be associated with big problems if you, as a Dane, want to create something that is aiming at becoming the best in the world. If you look at those Danes who are in the world elite within their fields, they often encounter a lot of resistance on the domestic front. If ten years ago, anyone would have had the temerity to suggest that Denmark might have the best female tennis player in the world, most of us would have shaken our heads in disbelief. Impossible! To reach those kinds of heights is the reserve of the Americans, the British, and the Germans! Well, today Denmark has the international tennis star, Caroline Wozniacki; in my eyes, she is not at all being treated with the respect she deserves in her home country. Instead of being proud of her, we will start focusing obsessively on the things in which she is not successful. This rule also applied to my vision of creating the world's best handball team. Years back, if someone had said that we could create that kind of team, he would have been laughed out of the handball court and condescendingly been told that that is something for Germany or Spain—never tiny Denmark! And you might say that the naysayers unfortunately ended up being right.

In Carsten's Words
A few words about this and that

An inconsistent dictator

It is late morning and I am on my way up to Jesper's house to record some more material for our book. Throughout the meetings we have had, the mood has gradually become increasingly informal, and each time we meet, we spend more and more time discussing the small things that are so important in people's daily lives. We are sitting at the table in Jesper's living room, and I decide to bring up something I have noticed several times during the time we have worked on the book. In several of our recording sessions, we have been discussing some of the same topics, but several times I have noticed that—depending on when I ask about a certain topic—Jesper might say something different from one time to the next.

What are these inconsistencies about? It is interesting that you mention that. Throughout my career, I have often experienced that people reproach me for contradicting myself. In general, I don't regard such instances as inconsistencies but as a sign that I don't have problems changing my opinions when the factual basis for those opinions changes. In the so-called established business world, there are many who experience it as a personal defeat if, for some reason, they need to change their opinions. One should remember that everything is always changing. This means that I also need to readjust myself to what I see, feel, and hear. It is exactly because I have been capable of constantly realigning myself that I have been able to reach unusual results; therefore, the fact that I am not afraid of being inconsistent often turns into strength.

But in the business world and everywhere else, one of the first things you learn is to put together plans and budgets for your work. Isn't it kind of hard to make plans where you constantly have to be ready to change? When I was busy with AGK, there were many people who asked me: "Now, of course, you've drawn up a detailed business plan for how your handball club will grow, haven't you?" I always feel like taking a nap when I get those kinds of questions. If there is anything, with 100 percent certainty, I have *never* done for any of my projects, it's to produce a business plan. In all the years I have been part of the business world, I have seen literally thousands of business plans that have never come to fruition, and which have only been a waste of time and paper. Let's say you have some kind of product you want to launch; so you make a plan for what should happen over the next three years. Two days after the plan is launched, something suddenly happens that makes everything look different. It might be a competitor launching his own new product or there might be a spike in the US dollar exchange rate. Those kinds of unforeseen factors can impact all the aspects of your plan, and you may have to take three months' work and throw it straight in the trash can. It is no use setting yourself targets and then not being able to change both the course and the final destination midstream, sometimes multiple times. There is nothing wrong with that. I have often been in situations where I've had a board of directors around me who became very agitated and confused and complained that I was constantly changing course or changing my opinion. I repeatedly had to explain to them that I wasn't changing our course so much as constantly adapting to the world around us.

Can you give me a specific situation where you needed to be ready to change course rapidly? Yes, when I worked for Pandora, I specifically recall that I launched a special campaign for Christmas. After three days, I could tell that we were not getting the kinds of numbers for orders that I thought the campaign would generate. In that kind of situation, it's no use to sit behind your desk reviewing your business plan or initiating all kinds of studies. What I did was to put on my coat and go from customer to customer to talk to them to see why the products were not selling. After a couple of conversations with some of our jewelers, I could feel that we needed to tweak a few things ever so slightly to make things happen. I went back to our company and made the necessary changes. Then, we restarted our engines and that's how we managed to move sales through the roof up to Christmas. In order for those kinds of things to be possible, I must have an organization where I have the full freedom to implement changes rapidly as well as my employees' trust and confidence and support the moment I suddenly start changing things.

Now, of course, I have never been a chief executive. But isn't it pretty normal that you listen to your customers and adjust to the market accordingly? Not at the speeds I do it. A normal top executive would not dare to have an organization where he, based on his gut feeling, can change everything in a couple of hours. Once he discovers that something is wrong, he might convene a consultation committee and have various studies and analyses prepared to clarify the problem. The entire process takes perhaps two or three months, and then it is often too late. Sometimes I see people who, when I tell them something, look at me in a puzzled manner and tell me that last week I told them something completely different. Generally, I can only agree with them, but I also have to recognize the fact that one of my competitors just did this or that, that a certain bill is working its way through the legislature, or that I had to allocate some key employees to a different project. And that's why we constantly need to make adjustments. For an employee who doesn't necessarily have the same overview as me, it can easily seem pretty confusing to have a leader who is constantly moving in relation to the world around us and who expects that his company should be able to do the same. Most people are not made that way, and they want to be able to lock in their efforts and just focus on one spot without having to think about anything else. They will perhaps experience it as having control of their future. Maybe they'll do something that is without rhyme or reason, now that they have agreed to this or that plan. Well, that's what they are doing, come hell or high water. If they would pay slightly more attention, they would discover that in many cases it doesn't actually require much effort to sense what is happening in the world around you and to make adjustments. In most cases by far, the adjustments that are needed will be pretty small, but far too many decide not to make those adjustments because they are blinded by the plan they have put together.

The same principle applies to people's love lives. When two people in a relationship lose their energy, it is often about defining a framework for the relationship that is far too narrow. If the energy in a company or a relationship needs to remain strong, it must be kept alive and possess a degree of unpredictability. Yes. Perhaps this is a universal principle, and one I also applied when I worked with AGK. Back then, I had a very precise goal that was about producing the best handball team in the world, but even if I had a clearly defined goal I was still moving around the entire time. For example, while working with AGK I suddenly had the chance to become the owner of one of Germany's best handball clubs. During that same period, I also decided to move to Germany. As I was moving, I decided that now I would focus on the German team. Going forward, my Danish club would only function as a kind of feeder club where we developed talents that would have the opportunity to play for the German team. In 2010, a number of things happened in both the Danish and German clubs that created a completely new situation, and within a few days I decided to shift tactics and focus my primary energy on the Danish team.

You obviously do not find it difficult to make changes in the moment. But how do you feel about your future? Do you sometimes experience that you can sense what the future brings? As far as the future is concerned, I am usually a completely blank slate. For instance, if someone asked me if I would ever return to work for Pandora, I would not be able to give them a 100 percent answer. The fact is that I'll never have any way of knowing what the world has in store for me and what I'll be doing in five minutes. Even though it may sound absurd right now, I can also not say that I will never go back and assume a central role in Brøndby IF soccer. As I have said before, it is smart to be able to make clear-cut and rapid decisions, but to lock yourself into them is not particularly wise. That is why today I'm in a place where I love change, because change means that I have to be fully present and alert all the time.

With respect to what we talked about a little while ago— being able to create rapid change and, in doing so, keep a culture, a company, or a project alive. That is actually a piece of ancient wisdom, which I don't know if you're familiar with. Many years ago, I read that several old cultures had a form of governance that resembles our modern form of democracy. The strength of democracy is that it ensures that a kind of broad-based common sense is being maintained so that one madman can't suddenly steer society over a precipice. The weakness of democracy is that it may cause decision processes to clog up in cases of conflicts and endless debates. Therefore, in some democratic cultures, it was decided to change the form of governance when the wheels of democracy were clogged up, and they chose a dictator who would be given completely free reign for a year so that things could be cleaned up before the person in question would be automatically deposed again. If a dictator has social qualities, has his or her finger on the pulse, gives other people room, and if he or she has empathetic qualities, there is no doubt he could be a really good leader.

But what about you? Are you in reality not a leader who functions at his best when he can act as a dictator? What I usually joke that in my companies I always work with a kind of unenlightened despotism. For my projects, it's pretty rare that they are put in committee. I think many of the people around me believe that I'm good at delegating responsibility in places where I am not particularly strong myself. On the other hand, I'm also pretty autocratic in places where I feel that I am the best person to take responsibility and decisions. When we're in that domain, everyone around me will also be more than welcome to provide me with all kinds of information and input. But in the end, in those kinds of situations, I want it to be just me making the decisions.

Can you elaborate on the particular domain where only you make the decisions?
Oh, I'd say along general strategic lines. I leave almost everything else to others.

Finances and consumption

Okay, I've wanted to talk to you about your finances and your consumption several times. When I make purchases, I often look for sales. Once in a while it irritates me when I spend three minutes on figuring out which milk is a quarter cheaper than another. That time is wasted since I could have earned more than a quarter in three minutes—even as a store clerk stocking groceries. I guess what I'm really talking about is what economists refer to as opportunity cost. I'm wondering if you also look for sales in the supermarket when you have several hundred

million in profits from your company? For regular groceries I never pay any attention to prices. The sales I usually notice are the kinds where there are three packages for this or that price, and then I don't pay attention to whether it would've been cheaper to buy them individually. On the other hand, I sometimes spend a good deal of time shopping for airplane tickets on the Internet. For that, I have a number of principles that might seem irrational—for example, I will happily visit three different websites to save $75. If I can find a ticket to Mallorca for $130, I'm happy.

Otherwise, what is your relationship with money? I mean, do you carry around cash? Hmmm, this morning I actually looked in my wallet and discovered that all I had was $7. As we've discussed several times, money in itself is not particularly exciting to me. It's just something that's there and when I need to spend money, I just have a completely ordinary credit card. With my current life style, I can probably manage for around $400,000 a year. Since I started trading jewelry, I have only experienced problems with the coverage on my credit cards once, and that was when the tax authorities froze all my assets.

But how about before you had money? Well, back then my consumption was naturally a lot. But my relationship with money was about the same. In reality, I believe that my relationship with money is something many so-called ordinary business people might find a bit scary. For example, if I'm sitting across the table from someone who wants to sell me ads or something or other, I'll listen to what he has to say. And once he's finished, I'll say either yes or no. If I say "yes," the sales rep will often think that we're about to embark on a long negotiation and an extended process in which we need to discuss stuff. I never want to do that. Once I've said yes, I don't want to hear any more. At that point, a decision has been taken and we move on. If I've been given a price and felt that I've been presented with something I want, there's nothing more to talk about. Because I operate in this way, I've often frightened the life out of sales reps who have sold me insanely expensive things and where I did not want to talk any more about it after I've said yes. For example, I bought a house on Mallorca without thinking about it and without wanting to hear anything at all about the house. Before going to see the house, I had already investigated what I needed to know. I just told the broker to send me the papers and a key, and I'd make sure to transfer the funds within the next couple of days. The poor man was completely shell-shocked and couldn't comprehend what had just happened. All the long drawn-out processes that often arise around commercial transactions are irritating to me, because in reality they are not about much more than a fear of money. A valuable lesson is that money is not dangerous, and as long as there's money in your account, there's nothing to be afraid of.

But at the same time, you won't know how much money you have at a given time, right? That's true. In recent years, I've been asked several thousands of times, somewhat indelicately: "How much money do you have?" My most honest answer is that I have no idea, and I will never know. Some people also sometimes ask how much money I have in the bank. And when I tell them that I don't have a bank account, they can't fathom what I'm talking about.

Er, I don't either, in fact. What do you mean you don't have a bank account? I have a number of credit cards and then my mom makes sure that there are always sufficient funds to cover the cards. That is, I don't have a NetBank or something like that which I can access to see what my balance is. I don't need it, and it doesn't hold any interest for me. Moments ago I told you what my annual consumption is. I actually have no idea if that's really the case—honestly, I just tossed out that number. Maybe I'm spending ten times that amount.

Based on that, I guess I can conclude that you're probably not a gambling addict who likes to go to casinos. And you guessed right. Contests, the lotto, and those kinds of things mean nothing to me, because I'm neither anxious about losing nor excited about winning money. Those types of games often only appeal to people's greed, and if you're not greedy, you won't find any energy in those kinds of things. At the same time, I also think greed is one of those conditions that keep many people from earning a lot of money.

I was once thinking that having a lot of money at your disposal can be compared to finding an attractive partner. An attractive woman or man wants to be where he or she is allowed to be without drowning in his or her partner's feelings. That goes for money, too. It will go where there's freedom and space. That sounds like a very true principle. But as far as I'm concerned, I rarely pay attention to whether I'm attracting money or pushing money away. Actually, I very rarely see money as anything but numbers on a monitor or a piece of paper. In my businesses, I am very alert to whether we have enough cash on hand, but the money itself I never see. That the money is there is really only a symptom that I can do as I please.

Organizational housecleaning

Many people will be familiar with the television program with master chef, Gordon Ramsay, who will drop in to a restaurant that makes lousy food. For a couple of weeks, he is free to whip the entire restaurant into absolute top shape with his inexhaustible energy. That goes for every-thing—from the décor to staff morale and then of course the quality of the food. The way I see you, you could be a kind of organizational equivalent to Gordon Ramsay. If a television show was produced where you were let loose in an ordinary business, you would most likely quickly be able to make it take off in some extreme way. What do you see as most companies' problem; one that you'd focus on, if you were airlifted in to revolutionize sales? Well, that naturally depends on the organization. But in my own companies, I'd say that I spend around 80 percent of my attention on giving my sales force absolute optimal condi-tions to succeed. To me, it will always be the sales reps who are the star players of a company, and because they are the ones generating the sales, I'm incredibly biased in my focus on them. As with the players on my handball team, I'm al-ways working intensively on removing all imaginable ex-cuses a sales rep may have not to be successful. You'll often hear sales reps say that the packages are too big, something is too expensive, or that too much is being returned. My work is not about convincing my sales reps that they can manage it in spite of that; my work is to make it as easy as at possible to achieve success. If we compare this to the world of sports, it is about giving the sales rep an unobstructed run to the goal so that all he or she needs to do is give the ball a tiny push over the goal line. Naturally, you also need to make sure that the product you're selling is unique and of top quality. This means that there must be no hitches, none whatsoever, and when all that is in place and the sales rep is standing out in the customer's store, all the conditions must be in place for him or her to score. Unless the sales rep believes that the rest of the organization will help to clear the way so that he has an unobstructed path to the goal, we're going to have problems. And because I always think this way, I often find newly hired sales reps from other companies who are astonished at the work we do to help them reach incredible heights. That this kind of thing is possible is about having the rest of the organization making a gigantic effort to have everything ready at both the left and the right flanks of the sales rep.

When you work this way, you'll have sales reps who will grow at extreme rates and start to radiate a fantastic self-confidence. This means that they will begin to work miracles and close deals that get bigger and bigger every time. Simultaneously, you also need to be aware that in most companies there is a kind of competition between the branches of the organization that are its public face and the ones that work internally—that is, the front office and the back office. For example, I once had a sales rep who booked an order for $70,000, but we had $13,000 worth of product returns. In the front office, he was a hero—in the back office there was grumbling about all the extra work. One of the methods I personally use to solve this problem is to constantly involve our back office in what takes place in the front office. Neither of these two parts of the company must forget that they are totally interdependent, and in the back office, everyone must be made to feel that their success hinges on how good they are at freeing up the sales rep in front of the goal. In many major companies, the back office is something you almost expect will develop on its own. And when, after ten years, you have not given it any special attention, that's when things start to go wrong. When I hold talks, I sometimes ask the audience if they have ever heard of a company where almost nothing works but which could be sold for a billion dollars because it has a world-class bookkeeping department. Who would buy that kind of company? The fact is that a bookkeeping department is not difficult to set up. All companies, regardless of whether they sell butter, wooden posts, or napkins, have about the same structure. What is different and what will determine whether they will be successful is almost always what takes place out in the field.

Do rules apply to rule breakers?

In many ways, you're a kind of non-conformist. When you're a non-conformist, you break norms, and you'll always have a difficult time to follow the rules society has established. I have a difficult time with rules—if I bike at night, I'll drive without lights and often on the wrong

side of the road. **If I need to get into a place where people are lined up, I'll sometimes try to sneak up in line but only if can be done without getting discovered. How about you? If you're going to the movies, and you can see your way to get in for free, would you do it?** No. In that area, I'm the type who'd rather pay one time too many than one time too little. With respect to tips, I also have a tendency to be more generous that my girlfriend likes. The fact is that I'm actually far too nice and well-behaved to break rules. The only place where I'd have a difficult time with rules is with respect to speed limits. I love to drive fast, but generally, I don't like the battles that arise when you don't follow the rules. I think it's got to do with the fact that back when I was a child I was very shy and preferred to crawl along the wall, or so I've been told, rather than to stand out. Then, I didn't want to stand out from the crowd—I preferred not to dress differently than others and preferred that no one notice me.

It sounds like you've undergone quite a transformation. When did that change? It changed when I discovered that you need to stand out from the crowd to get results and since I'm incredibly results-oriented, there was no way around it.

That particular perspective is one that I don't think I've heard before... In other words, at your core, you're a nice boy who doesn't want to create a scene or make a fuss?
That's right. If I'm in a restaurant and the food is bad, it would never occur to me to send it back to the kitchen. And even if the meal wasn't good, I'll still give the waiter a good tip. If I'm dissatisfied with a restaurant, the only way I'll

punish it is by not coming back. By and large, it is very remote for me to stand up and bang the table if I don't get what I pay for.

So, you won't get angry of you get poor service after having paid a fortune for flying business class? No. Instead of spending energy on complaining, I will just not choose that airline in the future. If I'm asked if I'm satisfied, I'd be happy to let them know if I'm not. But unless I'm solicited for an opinion, it doesn't make sense for me to spend energy on it. What does annoy me is when people with money become arrogant and demanding. I fully accept whenever I am told that, regrettably, I can't have what I had expected.

With respect to banging on the table or making a scene, the world of sports is an interesting study. There, feelings often rise to the top, and you often see coaches or players who shout and scream when their team is playing. Don't you ever do that? That, too, is something I would never dream of. When I like a team, I will always support them 100 percent—but without shouting and slinging mud at the opponents. I've also never bawled out a player if he didn't do his best.

What about referees? You don't shout at them? Oh, I stopped doing that around the time I stopped as a junior player. Back then, I discovered that this kind of behavior actually damaged the team more than it benefitted it. You see, it's not that I don't want to... the fact is that I always had a burning desire to win and increase the team's chances of winning. So, that's one bad habit I had to put on the shelf.

What do you mean? How can you harm your team by shouting? It doesn't matter if we're talking sports or business. Shouting and screaming are signs of weakness. If you have a burning desire to win, it's no use showing signs of weakness. Regardless of whether it's about sports or business, I have a basic philosophy that I adhere to: We must always do our homework much better than our opponents. That means that we will have trained the hardest and be the ones who come most well-prepared. If it is a business, we'll be the ones with the best product, the best materials, the best employees, etc. All the homework needs to be done before you enter the arena, and it needs to be done 100 percent perfectly. I almost get nauseous when someone says that they lost a game because they didn't have enough time to train. Hearing that kind of talk from me, my employees, and my handball team would be completely unthinkable. If we go on the court, to a tradeshow, or a meeting with a customer, we will always be prepared to the tips of our fingers. So, if we happen to meet an opponent and we lose, we need to go back to the drawing board and start doing our homework even better so that we can win the next time.

So, you think it's absurd when you see a coach standing by the sideline shouting? Yes, I do. If the coach and the team had prepared better, there would likely not be any reason to shout. Apart from that, losing your temper is not a sign of a winner's mentality.

You're talking a lot about the winner's mentality. But how do you feel about losing? I have an incredibly bad time with losing. All the way up until I was a teenager, I would sometimes tear up if I played handball and my team was losing. It is difficult for me to imagine anything worse than losing. And that's why, sometimes, I would rather not play a match than risk losing. With age, I have become better at not letting my emotions getting the better of me. If you want to win, it's no use walking around with your emotions on your sleeve. This makes you an open book to your opponents. In reality, it means that it will be even easier for them to prevail. I love to win but too much disgust with the prospect of losing can actually cause you to lose more easily. Today, it's no longer the fear of losing that propels me but, to a far greater extent, my joy in winning—that's my motivating force.

Knowing millionaires can be expensive

Some of the people I know who have a lot of money have become some of the most expensive acquaintances I have. The problem is that they attract others who want a share of their money. To show that I don't belong to that category, I often end up paying if I go out to eat with one of them. Since people with a lot of money often have expensive habits, I sometimes get cleaned out because they chose the restaurant. That is an area to which I've given a lot of thought. If I hold an event, invite people to a restaurant, or stuff like that, I often make arrangements to ensure that everyone has peace of mind with respect to the financial aspect.

How do you do that? As with so many other areas in life, I make a big deal out of being well-prepared—and if you are, you can go far. For example, if I take a group to a restaurant, I will usually make sure that they already have my credit card on file or that they send a bill afterward. Once my guests know that that's how it works, they will relax and we'll get far more out of being together.

So, it doesn't mean anything to you whether or not the people you're with have money? No, of course not. Last week I was out with an old friend who kept telling me about his wealthy business connections. I finally told him that I didn't want to hear any more because people with money do not interest me in themselves. What does interest me is *what* they do with their money. If they have earned many hundreds of millions of dollars doing something they don't live and breathe for, it is all completely irrelevant. One of the reasons money is uninteresting is that it easily shifts the focus from what is really important. For example, if I am planning an event at a hotel, all I am focused on is that the event will be excellent. If I start to put finances into the mix, I might easily forget what the matter at hand is really about. When I work on creating that kind of stuff, I don't look at the bill at all and usually don't ask what it costs. However, what is of critical importance to me is that the event was successful. For instance, when I did the world's biggest handball event in Copenhagen, at no point in time did I ever look at or worry about what it cost to arrange.

But what if you and some friends go out to eat? Do you always pick up the check? No. It varies a great deal who pays. Generally, it is the person responsible for inviting me or the host who pays, but I am well aware that it might be difficult for others to be with someone who is very wealthy. In fact, some people might even be downright uncomfortable with that. But I think I'm usually pretty good at making sure that it never becomes a topic of discussion. To be good at that, you need to help others remove their focus on money. Because I think this way, I often create situations where, for example, the tax authorities might have a difficult time understanding my motive for defining a specific activity as a business promotion and thereby tax deductible. For example, some time ago I was in a situation where I was looking to recruit a certain top executive as well as two sales directors who had accomplished quite extraordinary results. My sister and I took some meetings with them, but whenever the topic of their working for us was broached, nothing ever happened. As I got to know the three guys better, I invited them out for an evening at a restaurant, nightclub, etc. While we were partying and having fun, it was no problem for me to make the necessary agreements with all three of them. The next day I wrote my sister that everything was in place. She then contacted them to draw up contracts, and not long after that, they were working for us. With respect to our collaboration within the family, my task is to go around sowing the necessary seeds; my sister will then prepare the contracts and have the agreements formalized. The evening I took out the three guys on the town, I didn't give a thought to what it cost. All I thought about was to create a fantastic evening. If I were to guess, I'd say that the evening perhaps set us back around $27,000. If instead I had used a headhunter, the whole thing could easily have cost me ten to 20 times that amount.

On playing in your own league

Now, since you have such a hard time losing, do you spend a lot of time analyzing and studying your opponents or competitors? No. Regardless of whether I am working on developing a business or a sports team, I almost never spend time on that. If you are dedicated and work hard at getting the best out of what's available to you, competitors are really not particularly important. In other words, my point of departure is always that what I do should be in a league of its own. When you play in your own league, there is no reason to speculate about what your competitors are doing—no reason to think about which products they are developing, or analyze how they set up their pricing or marketing strategies. If you're playing in your own league, there are other things that are important. And at the same time, by thinking in this way, you create a state around your product and your team that means that others will not try to compete with you. Often they'll shrug and start to think: "Well, they are so far beyond us that there is nothing we can do about them." Generally, it is about creating absolute superiority in everything you do while realizing that it has consequences. I think it was President Harry Truman who said, "If you want a dog in Washington, get a dog." The fact is that it is always cold at the top. My suggestion is that if you have your heart set on having lots of friends, don't go for number one—try a step further down the ladder. If you're okay with only having as your friends the people on your team or in your company, it will become number one, which in turn will let you play in your own league. This was part of the philosophy that made AGK grow. Quite quickly, no one doubted that we were always running our own unique show. I never thought about which players the other teams were contemplating buying. My fundamental approach was always that it was more important to take an interest in which players *we* were buying and what the significance would be for our team. The way I saw it, it was not so important which players the other teams sent on the court, because they did not have the same winner DNA as we did and because they were unable to create the same conditions for their players that we could. That's why we would always win, no matter what moves other teams came up with. This meant that many of the teams we met had lost already before the referee could blow the whistle—they just didn't know it yet.

The Business Adventure Continues

New Horizons: Endless Jewelry

On creating most cherished possessions and conquering the world

Some of what I love most about working with jewelry is that it is designed to create great energy. Jewelry is not a product you need for survival; its purpose is to create joy and other positive states. It gave me no joy or pleasure—as I took my leave from Pandora—to sign a non-compete clause that I would refrain from working in the industry until 2013. With Pandora behind me, I readied myself for a long break from the jewelry industry where I would have time to focus on other things. Even though all my former customers had now become Pandora's, I could also see what my efforts as a visible leader up until 2011 had meant. Every time I met my customers from that time, they would always ask me when we could get going again, that they were pretty upset about what had happened, or they asked me when I would get back in the game with my own product. This was confirmation to me of the incredible strength there is in not cultivating "systems thinking," but to be bold enough to create something that is more organic and alive and built on the desire to give. The sales channel for jewelry I had created was not built on studies or analyses designed to maximize profits but on a desire to generate relationships, and it had no expiration date. If one day I were to get back into the industry, I would be able to reactivate my entire network in the six major European countries I had cultivated in just a few months. Most, by far, would not even need to know what product I wanted to sell them; they would just be glad that their old informal fun guy and jewelry big gun was back on track. Of course, Pandora's new management was fully aware of this, and it was also not hard to figure out that they, to put it mildly, were freaking out at the prospect of my re-entry into the business. As soon as my non-compete clause had expired, I would pop out like a troll in a box—a Pandora's Box. My old employees and my customers knew everything about my way of working and had always enjoyed it. They would stand ready in the wings and then jump on board my organization if one day I should choose to revive it.

When we reached June 2013, I was once more ready to start up. Before we reached that point, however, my mom and sister had already made all the introductory maneuvers required to reactivate our good old KASI Group. They had also actively entered the jewelry industry and had come up with KASI Group's own collection; a collection that would be traded under the title "Endless Jewelry." After the takeover of Pandora, the new management team had, as mentioned previously, been busy moving toward becoming a more exclusive brand. Our new collection was designed by Christina Hembo and was not only created to fill the vacuum Pandora left as a result of their new strategy. It was also a product of high quality that was simultaneously the natural continuation of the direction Pandora should have gone in the development of their brand. In 2013, we were ready with a collection I am sure will become even bigger than Pandora if it has the right kind of distribution.

This time we are the owners of the product we sell, and we can work without either a ceiling or limits. When the news that we were ready to re-enter the jewelry industry made its way into the media, former employees and customers who wanted to take part immediately started pouring in. The team that introduced Endless Jewelry on the German market was almost identical with the team that years back had introduced Pandora. Both my mom and sister had imagined that they would start slowly and quietly until I could join them, but it soon turned out that the whole thing just shot right into the stratosphere. The experiences we had had with Pandora—the positive as well as they negative— gave us an extraordinary motivation to make things happen again, and this time we could work at a far greater scale. Based on that, I also quite quickly started feeling a certain gratitude that Pandora's management team and I had parted ways. If that had not happened, I would be limited to only selling jewelry in five European countries for the rest of my life. Now, the whole world was open to us, and I could finally live out one of my dreams—that is, to come to the United States and from there, out into the rest of the world. The time had come to rev up the turbines without being held back by contracts or a logic-driven management team. Thus, Endless Jewelry not only became the title of the family's new collection but also a title that quite clearly described our vision for the collection's distribution. In other words, nobody can stop us—even if some day I might get the idea of selling Endless Jewelry on the South Pole, the moon, or in other solar systems.

With respect to Europe, my expectation was that we could jump right back into the game. With the knowledge, experience, and the image that I, by now, had acquired in the business, I had a completely new power. As far as Endless Jewelry was concerned, I started out with a gut feeling of being world champions right from the start. That is something customers, staff, and sales reps can sense. Apart from this, my entire network was ready, and the support of our customers meant that many things happened more or less by themselves. However, it was a big challenge for me to get the Pandora blood out of my veins. The Pandora I had known years back was my child, which I loved more than anything. Even now, three years after I have let go of Pandora, I could still feel the energy and the love that were there. To see Endless Jewelry starting up and feel the excited anticipation of customers and employees was not only a vindication but also an indication that the time had come to let go completely and move on. This time, I could not be hijacked and was able to continue with the exciting growth process that I was in the middle of until Pandora was acquired.

One thing many people have asked me during the launch of Endless Jewelry is where the idea for the name of the new collection came from. The answer is that back in 2007 I thought that this name would be just the right name for a jewelry collection. I had it registered for later use and had no doubt what our new brand would be called once we started up again. Endless Jewelry was not only a name that described our collection but also a very precise description of the collection's distribution, our energy as distributors, as well as the philosophy on which my way of working is based. When I start a new project it is always about creating a space of endlessness, with no ceiling, no walls, no floor, and no specific goal. In that way, my perspective becomes endless at all levels. For my Endless Jewelry journey, that means that I do not know where I am going or what will happen. The future will be shrouded in precisely the kind of uncertainty I need to keep up my heart rate, my energy, and my zeal at their peaks.

When people sense the incredible energy we are generating, they will liven up and grow with us. As with a wood stove, it is about getting the temperature hot enough so that the fire can feed on itself as long as you keep throwing in logs. What happened with Pandora when it was acquired by the equity fund was that the fire in the stove died down and that could naturally be seen in the company's accounts immediately. Conditions that cannot be quantified—such as energy, pulse, and dynamism—thus became completely central in building up the new organization. Of course, many of the people I took with me to Endless Jewelry came from Pandora. But I also realized how important it was also to bring people on board from outside the industry who could give us fresh perspectives on certain aspects of the business. It was actually interesting to see how these new people often felt the pulse and excitement far more acutely than those who came over from Pandora and who were already familiar with the energy and heartbeat of how we work. Some of the new people quickly became so dedicated to our "cause" that, in sheer excitement, they were champing at the bit to get to work at six in the morning and to work straight into the very late hours of the evening. By combining new employees with my former colleagues in Endless Jewelry, I quickly learned that I could create a very exciting dynamism.

With respect to Europe, it took me several years to get Pandora placed in just the right locations. On June 1, 2013, I was ready to get to work, and on the first day I contacted the leading store chains in Germany. One was Christ, Europe's biggest jewelry chain. The chain has stores in 210 locations in Germany in the very best locations. Then, there were the two department chains, Kaufhof and Karstadt. The former has 105 stores, the latter 85, and the last chain—Kraemer—has about 40 stores. Because I have an extraordinarily good relationship with the people there, I quite quickly closed a contract with Kraemer. If I had arrived with a consignment of my old underwear and asked them to put it in their display windows, I have little doubt they would have said yes—that is the nature of our relationship. That is why this was a completely natural place to start; and true enough, the jewelry was soon in all 40 of their stores. Then, I started on the other three. And, as I was sitting at the conference table with the buyer from Christ, she said:

"I'm so happy to see you! I thought you were angry with me."

"Angry at you?" I said. "Why on earth would I be angry with you?"

"I just saw Endless Jewelry over at Kraemer," she said, "so I was starting to wonder what I had done since you weren't offering it to me."

Naturally, I knew quite well that I was well-established in the European jewelry world, but that I was *that* well-established was beyond my wildest imagination. It took me a moment to recover before I could offer my excuses and could explain myself: "Well, you see," I said, "I have a pretty close relationship with the buyer at Kraemer who visits me privately and who comes to the parties I do in Mallorca."

"Well, I could do that, too!" she exclaimed. "Just let me know when to come down."

I had arrived at our meeting alone with my bag from Endless Jewelry. The thing was that during that entire meeting, I never actually managed to get the jewelry out of the bag—that is how busily we were chatting. What we discussed was actually far more interesting: We talked about management and sales philosophies, about ways of thinking about product distribution, about human values, and about personal matters. Finally, we also had a long talk about Pandora's current transactions, which had really rattled her and her people. During our discussion, in spite of everything that had happened, I realized I still had warm feelings for Pandora and its employees and even found myself defending them. I smoothed things out and explained that Pandora was just doing whatever they needed to do, but it is clear to everyone that they no longer had a visionary management team present in the field. It is only natural to expect a certain degree of neglect and misallocation of resources. As the saying goes, no management or organization can be obligated beyond their abilities.

On my way home, I was still a bit overwhelmed that the buyer from Europe's largest jewelry chain had taken Endless Jewelry into her stores without even seeing the product.

The more I thought about it, the more obvious it became that it might not be so strange after all. The fact is that it was I who gave them Pandora and that meant that, for many years, I had contributed to the chain's earning cascades of money on charm jewelry.

In June 2013, while most people were on vacation, I signed up all the major German jewelry chains with all their stores as customers of Endless Jewelry. I doubt if a similarly rapid piece of sales work has ever been accomplished. Christ subsequently requested that we start up by testing the jewelry in 20 of their stores to see if they would sell. I rejected that outright, telling them that the jewelry had already been tested and that I would need *all* of their 210 stores. They accepted and as of October 15, 2013, the jewelry was out in all their stores. After that, it was quite easy to go across the street to the other chains and individual stores to tell them that Christ was now a dealer of Endless Jewelry. There was little doubt as to their next steps.

Throughout my life, I have been accused of many things, but I do not think anyone has ever accused me of being a pessimist. Paradoxically, for once, it turned out that I had been too pessimistic in my vision of how fast we could set up distribution agreements for Endless Jewelry in Germany. After only a few months' work, we had an extremely effective distribution network in place. Within that same period, 635 stores dealing Endless Jewelry had been added, and in addition to this, we were busy opening 14 Endless Jewelry stores—in other words, specialty stores that would only display and sell Endless Jewelry. All the leading European fashion magazines had full-page ads with our jewelry, and my people had been successful in placing Endless Jewelry in the ultimate product-moving magazine category: "must-haves." Many say that fashion magazines have impenetrable divides between their advertising departments and their editorial departments. That is not quite true. When you start throwing millions in ads at a fashion magazine, they know you are serious. The editors start taking a natural interest in what you are doing. In this way, we quite easily received a number of very fine editorials and several forms of product placement. The campaigns and the publicity that were generated on that basis fed on their own momentum, which gave the stores even greater motivation to take in Endless Jewelry.

As a small curiosity, I should mention that—after Endless Jewelry had managed to get into more than 600 stores—we reached the so-called tipping point, the point at which we received the message that everyone in that industry longs for: Customers were now starting to ask for Endless Jewelry bracelets. That is the culmination of a process that requires enormous preparatory work. To orchestrate a process like the one I am describing here may not sound like rocket science, but it does require very broad knowledge and expertise, as well as a number of rare human qualities. Partially, you naturally need to be an accomplished merchant who can go out to your suppliers and put in place the proper payment terms and conditions. In my work with Endless Jewelry, this model was quite simple. Fundamentally, it is about arranging with our production facilities that we need a 60-day payment deadline. After that, we sell the product and get the money in the cash register before we pay our supplier. Of course, many people can figure out how to do that; that is not what propels you into the world elite. What does propel you is storytelling, being a good leader, and being a motivator who not only has a vision but who can and will go all the way. A different and important quality is about being a brand creator. As far as Endless Jewelry is concerned, we are not talking about a product that, like Pandora, *grew* into a brand, but a collection that was *born* to be a brand. In everything I do, in all my thoughts and all the decisions I take, I therefore keep in mind what kind of brand we are dealing with. In short, again, it is about working across the four channels I also utilized in my work with Pandora. As a company, we need to create fantastic energy and have it channeled out into the organization. From there, it needs to go further out to our sales reps, out into stores, and from there, out to our customers.

Thus, in order to succeed with Endless Jewelry, I need a number of specific qualities but also I need to be present in many areas. It is about being present and involved with your customers, with your colleagues, with your sales reps, while also being present in all areas in the media and in the public consciousness. The sales representatives need to realize that what they have is not just a job; they are representing a way of thinking and creating a life style. They need to be kept fully motivated and up-to-date in all the most important areas. They need to know where their products are currently being profiled in the media, which new dealers have come onboard, who has been hired at the company's headquarters, what his or her name is, and who he or she is. With respect to the latter, this is the most difficult discipline in the world: "long-distance management." It is the challenge of keeping our objective in sight; making sure that the sales reps are made to feel that their management team is close by, that management has their backs, and that it is always ready, willing, and able to go out to talk with sales reps and customers about how things are going.

With respect to my sales reps, I am also never afraid of showing them that I understand that there is nothing more difficult in this world than getting a customer to sign on the dotted line. Most people are ready to indulge in all kinds of procrastination to avoid the moment the order is signed, the so-called "moment of truth." This is the moment where everything will be revealed: You will find out if you have created a strong relationship; if you have been convincing; if your self-esteem is in order; and generally, if everything you stand for as a professional is worth a nickel. As any sales rep will tell you, to stand out there and get that order on the pad is simply the greatest kick you can have. Once you have made the agreement with the customer, you are in a state of joy—but you are also aware that this is the moment where the real work starts. Now, the customer has been convinced, and the moment has arrived where you need to live up to all the promises you made while also keeping the energy going. The time has come to bombard the customer with information about how important your products are. He or she needs to be offered all forms of merchandise—from boxes, to flyers, display cases, adhesive stickers for road shows, parties, and personal interactions— anything and everything that will help them help you. Beyond this, you should not be able to open a fashion magazine without finding advertisements for the product, editorial mentions, or various projects such as, for example, our large scale advertising campaign running on TV in Germany around Easter and on Mother's Day."

As the reader has probably understood by now, I do not go half-way with anything. One of the places where this is very evident is when I hold parties. If I am obsessed with details when I work, I am doubly obsessed with details when I arrange parties. There is no hotter topic of conversation in the German jewelry industry than the parties I hold at the big trade shows. The two large suppliers, Pandora and Thomas Sabo, apparently decided that they no longer wanted to attend the last large trade show in Germany. This year, when they heard I was back in the game and was planning on participating in the trade show, they rushed in to re-register. They were naturally afraid that I would steal the spotlight. The fact is that regardless of whether or not they show up, they will have a very difficult time preventing me from stealing the show. The fact is that at those kinds of conventions, it is *always* me who holds the party everyone talks about afterward. It will be a gigantic show, with partying all night, in huge rooms on several different floors. Of course, it is my people who will execute the general structure, but I am the one supplying the little tweaks that will make the party an unforgettable experience.

In previous years, we have done a gold/black themed party, a flower power party, and themes that have tapped into a current trend—themes that mean that everyone is always looking forward to seeing what we have come up with this time. Our parties always feature a number of surprise elements, but we also keep a number of fixed items on the agenda. It is about getting as many people on stage as possible and to create the infectious excitement Endless Jewelry represents, and that will lead to our becoming the world's largest brand. Perhaps we will announce the most beautiful jeweler, the jeweler with the fastest business growth, the one that has created the most amazing Endless Jewelry display, etc. There will be artists entertaining, waiting staff, theater, drinks as far as the eye can see, and the bar will truly be Endless—both with respect to contents and closing hours. The bar servers are not just staff from Endless Jewelry slinging drinks across the bar but professional cocktail mixers who know what it takes. And it is not just music booming from loudspeakers, but the perfect Café Del Mar lounge music, great lighting and energy, and a fantastic mood and ambience. Everything will be thought out to the last detail, so that everyone will feel completely at ease. We usually recommend, only half-tongue in cheek, that suppliers take precautions to man their booths with emergency staff until noon the next day.

When we execute parties like this, we also go to great lengths to show all our employees how we do things at Endless Jewelry. I witnessed this myself when I did the first major kickoff for our new British sales rep team in Birmingham, England. The framework had been set by three very capable and experienced guys who knew the business well, but who apparently did not know me particularly well. Honestly, things had not gone exactly the way I wanted. The three well-meaning guys had booked us into a Hilton hotel, had offered coffee and cake for the afternoon, and then booked some kind of standard, middle-of-the-road dinner for everyone in the evening. At some point during the day, I sat down with them and asked how they had felt when they had visited me. Everyone smiled—they always had a fantastic time, thank you for asking.

"You always think of everything," one of them said, and one of the others added, "It doesn't matter if you want a hot dog or something like that at midnight. There it is, a hot dog."

"Right," I said. "Well, we're about to hold a meeting for 38 potential new sales reps. These are people who, for the next many years, will be responsible for ensuring that you will be successful with what you guys are trying to start up in Britain. You should see it as the most important meeting and the most important day of your entire lives. How do you guys think things are going?"

"Why…" they said nodding to each other. "Everyone seems happy and interested. So, that's a good sign!"

"So, who is going to save things and make sure things go well?" I asked rhetorically.

"There is no doubt about it—you," they replied. "When you go on stage, what you do is completely special; none of us can do that."

"Fine," I said obligingly, "so where is the candy? Where is the popcorn machine? Where are the wraps? There is nothing more irritating than sitting at a meeting like that and then getting hungry. Remember, everyone needs to be comfortable so they'll be happy and energized by being in our company; and, talking about being energized, where's the Red Bull?" They looked at each other perplexed. I continued: "As far as I recall, they don't do doping tests in the jewelry industry and, if there is anything that will perk you up and create energy, it's Red Bull. Don't be afraid to give our people Red Bull! There won't be any representatives from some jewelry association traipsing in to test the audience afterward to see if they are doped. So, start pouring!"

At one point during the day, I made the relevant arrangement and during one of the breaks, ice-cold Red Bulls were served to all the sales reps. Generally, sales reps are not the most unconventional individuals. In most cases, they are nice respectable people who go to work dressed in jackets and ties. They are used to working within a formal framework. It does not take much to wake them up and to make them realize that what is going on is something completely unique. When Red Bull was served at a jewelry meeting where the outlook was for a few cookies and coffee, the mood was lifted tremendously. As everyone was drinking Red Bull, I held up one of the Endless Jewelry tags which everyone had received at the entrance and told them that by showing the tag, people would get free drinks at the bar for the rest of the evening and night. In addition, the hotel naturally ensured that that evening's soccer match between England and Scotland was shown in the bar. After the match, we had time for some completely informal interaction.

When the party ended, they had all had a fantastic day and night, and they were all fully motivated. Now they knew that by working for me, you would have many more great experiences to look forward to. In the end, when we tallied the results, it turned out that all the 38 sales reps present wanted to represent Endless Jewelry's products. We only needed 20, and it was difficult to pick from this fired-up crowd. But once that was done, those 20 were taken to Mallorca to develop a great mood and to warm them up some more before sending them out to sell.

For an organization, you might say that sales representatives are like satellites. Out in the field, you easily feel disconnected from the daily life and routine of the back office. Therefore, you should never overlook an opportunity to pamper them—and I mean really pamper them. When I gather sales reps for meetings and an overnight stay is needed, there will always be a small goodie bag in the hotel room with chocolates, two small bottles of vodka, a pack of aspirins and two bottles of water as well as a personal greeting from my sister saying how much we are looking forward to spending time with them. That is the kind of area where many companies go wrong, because they do not love those little details that get them to stand out from the crowd. To me, the primary obligation of a business is not to earn money but to create an opportunity to shower love on customers and colleagues, and when everything forms a synthesis, the financial success will come all by itself. If you do that, and if you do it right, you can transform a small bracelet with charms into a billion-dollar business.

As I mentioned, Endless Jewelry has had the wind in our sails from its inception and when something moves ahead at those speeds, there is always a danger people will start thinking: "Wow, things are going really well! I guess we can take it easy for a bit." Success can be intoxicating, but it can also turn into a pretext for doing nothing. Regardless of what happens, I constantly remind people that what we are experiencing right now is nothing compared to what we *want* to experience. We can always become *much* better; we will always need *more* customers; and we can always work *much* faster. Viewed from a sports perspective, things become a bit clearer. If you have a sports team that is about to play another, not very good team, many will have a tendency to lower their expectations and energy level. That does not work for me. Regardless of how poor, unengaged, and talentless our opponents are, this will not affect our attitude to things. Once we walk onto the pitch—no matter if it is in a sports arena or the business world—we will play to our full potential *every single* time. There will always be someone ready to suggest: "But, come on, once in a while it's okay to play so-so." It does not matter if we are talking sports or business. That kind of mentality is destructive, because it infects everyone around you—across all channels, and eventually it also affects the consumer. According to my philosophy, there are only two options: You either do your best or do not do it at all. If our team can win by 15 goals, why settle for a win by eight?

When launching Endless Jewelry in the United States, I had a business meeting with my American partners in Miami. At the meeting, they told me that they had set a target for Endless Jewelry to be stocked in 2,500–3,000 stores across the United States. I asked them how they had arrived at that particular number. They told me that is the number of stores our competitors, Fossil and Pandora, have.

"Okay," I told them, "so now we know that is *not* the number we'll be aiming for. Rule number 1 always is that there's no reason to be like everyone else. So, instead, let's base our efforts on figuring out where *we* want to set the ceiling." This made all my new partners perk up their ears, and now that I had their full attention, I continued: "There's no reason whatsoever to pat each other on the back, thinking everything is dandy and then later discovering that the potential was actually much greater than our ambitions. In Germany, there are currently around 1,400 stores that stock Endless Jewelry—but the United States is about five times bigger than Germany, with sales 14 times higher. Why should we settle on fewer than 3,000 customers? That would mean leaving a *huge* vacuum of unused potential on the store counters! I propose that we put 150 sales representatives in the field and get Endless Jewelry into between 5,000 and 7,000 stores."

That made my partners fall off their chairs.

"Can you launch at that kind of rate?!" they exclaimed. "We've never seen anyone go that aggressively into a new market before. You should also remember that there are many players in the market over here, and there are many copycats."

"Yeah, I've heard," I said, "but once *we* enter the market we'll blow all the copies to kingdom come. I did that with Pandora in Germany. If Pandora had tried to stay ahead of the curve here in the United States, they would have done the same. The fact is that Pandora has been asleep at the wheel for a long time now!"

"But how do we get rid of the copy products?" they asked.

"Well, the only place you shouldn't go after copy products is in court," I said. "Everywhere else we'll just need to kill them. For starters, our objective will be to start up in a format that means that there won't be any oxygen left for anyone trying to enter the market with copies of our products, The first thing we'll do is to create such good relationships with jewelers that we can tell them that they don't need to deal with anyone but us. When they see how we work with them and what we're willing to do for them in terms of marketing, service, etc., they'll quickly discover that they will have no need at all for the others. In addition to this, remember that Endless Jewelry is a brand. When the individual customer asks for one of our pieces of jewelry, it would be futile for the jeweler to try to find a copy at half the price. Our customer will naturally want the genuine article."

We talked things over for a while, and in the end, I finally told them the story of Phaeton. Phaeton was a limousine that was manufactured by VW. This was a fantastic car, luxury class, but it cost only half of what other limousines of the same quality cost. The question was if they could sell it. No… of course they couldn't! The fact was that no self-respecting businessman would drive a car purchased at a deep discount. What signal would that send to his peers? As mentioned, Endless Jewelry is a brand. You can copy the product itself, but all the stuff customers attribute to and associate with Endless Jewelry cannot be copied. Copies will be dead meat on arrival.

As we wrapped up the meeting, we agreed to launch Endless Jewelry in the United States as we had already done in

Germany. Our score board so far? We have moved six times as fast as Pandora did during its launch phase in Germany. The only difference between Germany and the United States is that our level of ambition in terms of sales is 14 times as big as it had been in Germany. Before our meeting ended, my American partners wanted to know if we should perhaps copy some of our competitors' most popular jewelry. Here, I had to repeat myself and end the meeting by reminding them that we do not do copies—we kill copies.

To launch a global brand like Endless Jewelry requires focus in a lot of different areas. However, nothing is more important than being able to maintain and channel a vision and have the people around you feel that what you are talking about can actually be accomplished. With respect to many of my employees, I tend to be quite a bit further ahead of them in vision. We all know that there are currently about 32 million women in Germany who know what Pandora is. We also know that all the new jewelers who are stocking Endless Jewelry have started to tell their customers that they should really have a look at the new collection from "the guy who launched Pandora." As when I started Pandora, I can already now close my eyes and see where Endless Jewelry will be in three years. You will be able to walk down the streets of Miami, Hamburg, London, or Paris wearing one of our bracelets. If you stop three random women, they will look at it and exclaim:

"Why, that's an Endless Jewelry bracelet!"

In Carsten's Words

Meeting the designer

On designing quality for a broad target group

One afternoon I sat down to chat with Christina Hembo, the designer behind Endless Jewelry's collection, at Endless Jewelry's office. I decide to start by talking to her about love:

When you give jewelry to others, it is about love and warm feelings. What's your own relationship with the loving spirit? It takes up a lot of space in my life. In 2002, when I was studying design in London, I met my husband Claus completely by accident in the street. We are very different but we have a lot of the same dreams and ways of looking at life. We have been a great team since we met—both privately and in terms of work.

How did you start out as a designer? About ten years ago, I became very inspired by Ryan Air. Their idea was to deliver a luxury product at incredibly low prices. Claus's background is in the watch industry, and I have always been interested in jewelry. We started talking about how we might go about producing a series of classic, feminine Swiss watches with genuine gems for people on a regular income. Even if the prices needed to be low, we didn't want to compromise on quality. We were talking about a product that was designed from scratch. Each design was hand drawn and developed individually, and when we took the watches around, they became a gigantic success. In fact, they're still selling today throughout the world. Later, we started to work on developing a watch band of sewn calf skin, which enabled women to transform the watch into a charm bracelet. It was the first time in the world that anyone had done designer jewelry with charms in genuine silver with genuine gems, which could also show the time. When we presented the concept to jewelers, they gave it an overwhelming reception, and it was subsequently a huge success—in terms of both design and sales.

Why do you think your customers love the things you and Claus are making? Women really like that we use genuine gems and other natural articles and that we are not into synthetic materials. At the same time, I don't think they are used to being able to get this kind of quality for what is a relatively modest sum. For example, we don't *glue* gemstones onto our jewelry. Instead, we set them by hand with grabbers in silver. This makes the jewelry much more durable. We are also very attentive to the fact that the entire concept needs to be practical. That's why all of our silver pendants are rhodinated so that they don't have to be constantly maintained and polished. The jewelry should also be easy to take off and put on, and it should be easy to exchange individual charms. As a woman, I know how important it is that you can manage it yourself when you put on your jewelry.

When did you partner up with the Nielsen family? Well, it was pretty obvious that we're an excellent match in terms of value. We have the same attitude toward a lot of things. Both my husband and I are passionate about sports, and we have, among other things, sponsored cycling teams. And as far as jewelry is concerned, Claus and I share Jesper's vision: It's about creating something unique that is not only tops in quality but also caters to a broad target group. When Jesper saw our concept, he didn't have a second's doubt that this was precisely what he'd been looking for.

Could you tell me about your process in designing your jewelry and pendants? Sure. I'm not the kind of person who can just sit down and the ideas will start pouring in. Instead, I'm greatly inspired by nature or by walking around town looking at designs. For example, to me, old classic cars are an inspirational gold mine: They often have myriads of small details that inspire me to create parallel designs. When I'm out walking, I'm always carrying around a sketchbook to quickly draft, write down, or draw an idea. In everything I create, it is always important to me that there is a history, an idea, or a thorough process behind it. To give you just one example, from my walks on the beach I will design an ocean theme with pendants based on starfish, fish, and dolphins. For that theme I'll use gemstones such as blue topaz as well as white and black diamonds and white sapphires. Everything is designed so that it'll be within the context of the leather band. This little pendant, for example, depicts a dolphin made to look as if it is swimming around the leather band. So, it's not just a pendant representing a dolphin, but a dolphin designed in relation specifically to the leather band. As you can see, we've paid quite a lot of attention to the design itself, but we've also taken great care to have it form part of a greater context of the band. If you keep turning around each pendant, you constantly discover new details. Here's another pendant with a freshwater pearl resting on a leaf. The leaf was one I spotted as I was strolling through the woods, and it just struck me how incredibly beautiful they would look together. When I do these kinds of pendants, I start by hand drawing them. Then I make a two-dimensional drawing on my computer. After that, I'll have a draftsman reproduce it with measurements, depth, and all the other details that are important to be able to actually manufacture the pieces. Each design has its own drawing and its own history based on an idea of not appealing to short-term trends in the market, but to last forever. In that way, to me, Endless Jewelry is just the right name. We are trying to create something that is not aligned with any particular fashion, but something that needs to be able to work in all cultures and places forever.

But what exactly is it with women and gemstones? Even though, as a culture, we're talking a lot about equality and that women and men need to be able to do the same kinds of things. Don't we shake our heads in exasperation when we hear songs like "Diamonds Are a Girl's Best Friend"? A woman knows that when a man gives her a genuine gemstone, it has symbolic value. It is symbolic of feelings and intentions that are genuine. A girlfriend once showed me a ring her boyfriend had given her a couple of years earlier. The ring had a little white stone. When I asked her what kind of stone it was, she told me that it probably wasn't genuine. One day, just for fun, we agreed to have the stone tested, and when my girlfriend discovered that it was in fact a *genuine* diamond, it had an incredibly positive effect on her relationship with her boyfriend. Previously, she didn't think he would spend that much on a stone, and now her emotional reaction was tied up with the symbolism represented by the stone. Even though feelings are naturally not created by diamonds alone, I still think that many women endow gemstones with a certain amount of importance.

It's interesting that gemstones are hard when the feelings they symbolize represent what is traditionally perceived as soft. How are those two connected? I think it's about how contrasts can sometimes play off of each other. My husband and I are also contrasts who have managed to come together. And there might be a great deal of strength in opposites attracting because together they represent a whole—like the symbolism of yin and yang.

Could I possibly ask you to give me a couple of final words about what you are doing these days? Right now I'm working on a series of pendants about children, pregnancy, and birth—so-called birthstones. Each month of the year will have a gemstone associated with it, but I'm also trying to work with the symbolism of having a baby—creating a sense of security, building a nest, creating calm, and about the energy that arises when a new child enters the world. Of course we are talking about an event that takes up enormous space in every mother's life. And I feel that it's an event that the mother's partner should mark by giving a genuine piece of jewelry to commemorate the birth of their shared joy: their child. These days I'm spending a lot of time just lingering on the moods surrounding birth and then letting the ideas and inspiration come to me that will then develop into individual designs. At the same time, I'm also working in other areas. Before you arrived, Claus and I just had a meeting with Jesper, and I jotted down some keywords with my upcoming collections' themes. Let me look in my notebook: I have nature, love, beach, Christmas, big city life, vacation, calm, colors, energy, flowers, animals, the universe, the sun, the moon, adventure, fairy tales, fairy, magic, frog, prince, and wizard. All these are areas where, I'm sure, many of the women who love Endless Jewelry can find symbolism; a symbolism that has personal significance to them.

In Carsten's Words

Visiting the family

On unity, acceptance, and taking pleasure in differences

We are in the process of wrapping up Jesper's book. But before sending it off to the printer, we have asked his father, mother, and sister to read it and give their comments. One evening while Jesper is in Mallorca, I go out to meet them at the parents' house right outside Copenhagen to talk to them about the book. Jesper's father, Jan, shows me in and, along with Jesper's mother, Dorthe, and his sister, Annette, we sit down at the living room table to discuss their thoughts on the book. Jan stands next to the table for a couple of minutes participating in the discussion before he retires, leaving the meeting to the rest of us. With respect to these kinds of meetings, it is evidently the women who do the talking.

So do you recognize Jesper in the book?
Annette: I've read the book twice now. I have to say, I'm very happy with the result. As I'm reading Jesper's story, I sense both his incredible curiosity about life and his honesty.

In the beginning when Jesper started talking about his relationship with you guys—frankly—I actually started doubting his honesty. For me, as well as for many others in our culture, it's hard to imagine that anyone can work alongside his family that way.

Dorthe: As a family, we are incredibly tight. We share everything with each other. But we are also incredibly different and very stubborn. Because of how different we are, the division of labor was actually completely natural. All four of us have always had respect for what each member had done and could contribute.

Annette: If we'd been identical, I'm pretty sure it would all have ended up as one big brawl. But since we are so different, it's hard to get in each other's way. You should also bear in mind that there are many other things going on in this family that have nothing to do with Jesper's business projects. Our entire lives, Jesper and I have been involved in helping our parents in various ways. At the same time, working has always taken up a lot of space in our family, so if one of us is really busy the others will be ready to step in. When Jesper had all those gas station marts, it was also completely natural for us to become involved there. In an extension of our other jobs, we have all helped out at the gas station marts—both at the cash register, doing inventory, cleaning, or other things. This, too, was the case when Jesper worked for the supermarket chain.

Dorthe: And when Annette went abroad to work in Croatia for the Ministry of Foreign Affairs, Jesper, Jan, and I went down to help her and to be part of what she was doing there during our vacations.

So, you never had any conflicts with your kids?
Dorthe: No. You hear so much stuff about teenagers rebelling against their parents, but we've never had any of that in our family.

Of course you've been fortunate enough to have a number of areas where your interests coincided with those of your kids. Here, I'm thinking mostly in terms of sports and music.
Dorthe: Yes. You could say that we've become part of everything our kids were interested in, but that's been a two-way street. In our family, we've always been able to share all our enthusiasms with each other—no matter what they were.

Jesper is a force of nature and has often made pretty direct statements in the media. Has anyone in the family ever cringed with embarrassment over the stuff he's done or said?
Dorthe: No—never, none of us has. We're all very different, but if one of us gets up and expresses a specific opinion, we'll always be ready to back each other up.

Annette: Actually, come to think of it, the only time I ever cringed was in the beginning when Jesper started to do things in Germany. He was so unbelievably bad at German—but he quite quickly got much better.

You're currently seeing Germany as the home for the group you've created, and that's where you'll start selling your new brand "Endless Jewelry." How do you feel about that?

Dorthe: Fantastic! My fingers are itching every morning to get started. Of course, we lost our baby, Pandora, and we were very sad about that. It may sound strange, but we never actually owned Pandora. But all our employees and customers have always experienced Pandora as ours. When Pandora was acquired, we lost all our influence in the organization, and we had to pull out. Because we were no longer able to be there for them, many of our employees felt rejected or disappointed. Now, we have our own product and can decide everything ourselves. That just gives you an indescribable energy and also the opportunity to get back to what we love.

Could you say a few words about what you are most looking forward to with respect to working with Endless Jewelry?
Dorthe: I'm already pretty far along with getting the business up and running properly, and I'm looking forward to continuing with that. Some of what excites me is designing systems so that we can manage our finances and the logistics aspect. Once the systems are ready, we will be able to just press a button for many of the very routine back end functions such as delivering goods, issuing invoices, and so on. Apart from that, I'm really looking forward to being surrounded by people who're all working together to achieve the same goal.

Annette: To me, it is also the thought of the collaborative aspect that attracts me the most. It'll be fantastic to get to work in the morning, to talk with your employees, to find solutions, and solve problems together. The family, once again, will be the one setting the agenda and pulling everything together. During the final days of Pandora, we were working in some kind of corporate three-ring circus where every little decision had to pass through a number of sluices which produced a ton of problems. The fact that we had to take directions from a management team with little to no understanding or comprehension of what was going on at the customer level meant that we often had to say no to our employees and customers. That's why I'm so excited about building a business that acts like a living organism where you'll be able to say "yes" to everything again. The new business will be dexterous and agile enough to allow people to make quick decisions without being bound hand and foot in red tape. That's where our family is right now: We have tons of experience, and it'll be exciting to see what happens once we can apply that experience again. We know exactly what we need to do and where we want to go. We have some idea of *how* to do it, and we know a lot about what *not* to do.

How much are you working on Endless Jewelry these days?

Dorthe: Quite a lot of hours actually. But it's not my plan to be quite as active as when I worked with Pandora. Back when we started with Pandora, I was 57 years old and worked from eight in the morning until ten at night. It was a great time, and I was so engaged that the work never became a chore. Lots of people were wondering about my passion for Pandora and couldn't understand why Jan and I were willing to forego our steady incomes and to mortgage our home to start up in the jewelry industry. We were supposed to have traveled and relaxed—and instead we decided to make this giant leap into this crazy project that would consume almost all the hours of the day.

Annette: When Jesper started, I had a nice, comfortable job as a lawyer in the public sector. There was great job security, and I had a nice tidy career path carved out. In that particular culture, there was complete puzzlement that I would resign to work alongside my family. Personally, I saw it as long-awaited opportunity to break out of my life as a wage slave and be able to shape my own life. That I'd be able to do it together with my family just made the prospect all the more attractive.

While working with Pandora, you were not able to sell jewelry in Denmark. Will you be doing that in the future?
Annette: No. As a jewelry market, Denmark is not interesting to us. If you imagine Jesper entering a jewelry store in Denmark, it won't be the jewelry seller the jeweler sees but the person the tabloids have created, and we don't want to spend our energy on that. The world is a big place and we will go out into the world to markets where we'll be recognized for what we can do, and we won't deal with all the stuff concocted by the press. What we know how to do is to sell, market, and distribute jewelry.

Stunt No. 10

Working Hard

On whether there might be a method for creating success after all

I started this book by saying that there is no recipe or method for creating success, but I realize that I have to qualify that statement. In reality, you could say that there is a method that quite a lot of people have a tendency to overlook. And that goes under the category of *working hard* and doing so from morning to night. If we were putting a recipe together for how doing something can be transformed into success, imagine that you have a company with 500 employees. As their management team, you can choose to do something extra for them, to make them feel appreciated and special and make sure they are happy doing their jobs and to create the conditions for experiencing success in their jobs. The latter is perhaps the biggest gift you can give an employee. For most people, salary can become almost irrelevant—as long as they are successful in the tasks they are solving. If you create a company with 500 employees who are given the feeling of being successful every time they start to work, that is when magic happens. The result is quite simply that everyone in the company will work a little harder and go a bit further than your competitors. If you give people the right framework so that they get a chance to feel involved and to feel what they are doing is both meaningful and contributing to an end goal, you barely have to ask them to give an extra hour at both ends of their workdays. That means we can set up an equation that, in its simplicity, looks like this:

500 employees + the right framework = 1,000 extra hours of work a day

This equation provides an insight into how I have created organizations or projects that have been able to constantly surprise and grow at a rate no one thought possible. When you are a big group of people who are all putting in a couple of hours extra a day, you will inevitably travel faster and further than other companies in the same timeframe. With respect to work, I have always felt like giving a little extra over and above what is required, and that easily spills over into your surroundings. That this is the case has to do with the fact that I come from a working class family. My dad was an electrician, and my mom was originally a kindergarten teacher. From the time I was tiny, I have never heard of anyone in or around my family who was afraid of getting their hands dirty—of working hard. At the same time, my family also consists of perfectionists. They will not just do the bare minimum but will always ensure that they not only go the extra mile but a couple of extra miles after that. It goes without saying that the basic product should be in perfect order; the customer knows and expects it to be delivered as agreed. Where you can make a difference is in the packaging itself and the details that may seem small but which mean the world and which we have always been very good at putting into place in our business models. What I always tell my employees is that they need to bring love into what they are doing. What that means can be completely different from customer to customer. But for our jewelry distribution, it might mean that, before closing up a box for a customer, putting two pieces of beautifully wrapped chocolates in the box resting on a card with our warmest greetings. It is the detail, the extra love, that little extra service—that is the kind of stuff I have always focused on. If you do that kind of thing consistently, you build up a relationship with your customer that might benefit you if, at one point, you make a mistake or promise the customer something that you might not be able to deliver. But it is also important to remember that you cannot cut corners by not delivering a basic product that is not up to scratch and then give your customer a bit extra at the other end to get things to work out. You must be able to deliver great, high-quality products, on-time shipping, and be a business partner that the customer can trust and who supports the customer in everything he or she does. Once that is in place and as you give that little extra push, that is when magic in business is being created.

As I regularly drive past our old offices at Pandora CWE, I have noticed a shift has taken place—one visible to the naked eye. From always being lit up when you drove past at ten or 11 at night, the lights are now out at around five in the afternoon. The fact that our employees had worked *that* much more before was not about someone forcing them to do overtime. No, it was about a certain *esprit de corps* and extra love of work. It is the resulting fulfillment and impulse that means that people want to give an extra effort. At the same, employees never sought recognition for working more. The reason our employees worked more was because they had become passionate about the tasks they were solving. But it is interesting to note that it is not the tasks in themselves that generate that passion, but the energy and presence created by a certain form of leadership. The day that presence disappeared, the magic went the same way, and this happened at the precise moment a streamlined and profit-oriented management assumed command.

Stunt No. 11

Taking Pleasure in the Future

On letting go, uncertainty, and looking forward to both large and small things

I recently talked about the future with my 15-year old son, David. His ambition is to do what I do, and he wanted to know which kind of business degree I thought he would need if one day he wanted to be a CEO. My reply was that he should not take any kind of business degree to do that. He needs to learn languages, lots of them. The rest he will pick up when he starts working at a company and gains some practical experience. The longer you stay in school and try to conform to expectations others set for you to learn pointless stuff, the more locked in you become. The problem is that you are becoming conditioned to spend your time on stuff that will not work in reality. For a company to survive in the future, it must be able to break out of the box of conformity and constantly be able to do the unexpected. When Steve Jobs once presented his vision of how we needed to move a lot of regular activities from the desktop computer to the telephone, I do not think Nokia and the other players took it seriously. That vision is what we currently know as the iPhone. Steve Jobs did not conceive of that idea by attending school and learning to think like everyone else, but through a long process where he gradually found the courage to think outside the box.

If I were to start a school, I would not fill up the students' heads with a lot of details about the past. Instead, I would teach them to embrace the future. Throughout my entire life I have spent very little time and effort on evaluating and documenting the past. No matter how you look at it, the past is always over and even if you can learn from the past, that past should not take up too much space. It may be a cliché, but it is still true: pleasures are greatest in anticipation. To wait for something to happen is really the most life-affirming state you can imagine. In my way of working, I am always excited to find out what will happen next, and that means that I am never afraid that things might go wrong. For example, when I worked with my handball team, I was never worried about whether we would win or lose a match. I always looked forward to winning but did so without fearing losing. That is how I have always felt about my business and that is why I easily come across as a winner already, even before the match has even started.

Looking forward to the future, embracing it, is one of the secrets of creating a winner's culture in a business. And once that has been created, it is never a disaster if you sometimes do not succeed. If you do happen to lose, it will almost be irrelevant since you are immediately getting ready to win the next match. When I am busy on a project, we never waste our time drawing up various scenarios for what might happen if things do not succeed. With me, you always work based on the idea that we have always prepared optimally and have nothing to fear. In reality, this if one of the areas that makes me see sports and business as two sides of the same coin. Most people can understand it if you are passionate about your work, but many have a difficult time understanding how you can be passionate about a certain sports team. The reason both sports and business fascinate me so much is that they feed on the same passion. It does not matter if it is sports or business: I am not particularly interested in *how* we will prevail over our competitors or *what* they do. What is most important is to create a fantastic team or a fantastic organization that will always perform optimally. If you succeed in performing optimally, you undergo a process of continuous growth—you might even become the best in the world—and from this position, financial success will usually just be a natural, almost unavoidable, outcome. In my son David, I see that he has already started showing the kind of passion I know myself. The passion he feels the strongest about also happens to be one of my passions—and that is the soccer club, FC Barcelona. When David talks about Barcelona's team, it is always very clear to me how strong his feelings are for this club. During the summer of 2013 when he and I were in Mallorca, he asked if we could go to the Spanish mainland to watch Barcelona train. David then found out when and where the players were training, at which point we flew over to Barcelona. At that time, I was naturally aware that he was very fond of Barcelona, but it still surprised me to see how much it meant to him to actually see the players train. I got tickets for us for the club's next home match.

On our way to FC Barcelona's home match, I marveled at David's joy in what we were on our way to experience. To be with him reminded me of the passion I used to have for the soccer club Brøndby IF. I always knew when and where they were playing. And it was of vital importance for me to see *all* of their matches, and I was incredibly nervous before the matches would start. To feel that way about your team is a completely special, intense, and fantastic sensation, but when David and I were on our way to the huge stadium in Barcelona, I also felt how far away I had come from Brøndby IF. The last times I had seen Brøndby IF play, I did not even have the energy to get out of my seat when they scored. By stepping into Camp Nou, FC Barcelona's cavernous stadium, and feel *that* energy, it was quite clear to me why my interest in Brøndby IF's soccer club had disappeared. Why would I be a supporter of a club that is currently only a shadow of its former self and wastes all its strength not on winning but on avoiding demotion? At Brøndby IF, the present management team is primarily concerned about the club being a financially responsible business. Sure, it needs to be that—but if that is its management's primary focus, that club will never rise again. The old Brøndby IF was a world that was parallel with my outlook on life and my philosophy; the new Brøndby IF has been hollowed out and, like Pandora, lost its pulse, its dynamism, and thereby its energy. Over a period of just a few years, my life had taken a completely unexpected turn in several areas. Not only did I have to let go of Brøndby IF and AGK, but also my Pandora. On the other hand, I have started a new life with FC Barcelona and Endless Jewelry and with this development, I have been set completely free from my native country—I am deeply grateful and ready to conquer the world.

Among the nearly 100,000 spectators at FC Barcelona's stadium, both David and I were in our element. Among the spectators, we found *all* kinds of people—from the old granddad of 86 years, to a group of friends on a trip, to a woman with her five children. FC Barcelona's fan culture is not only based on a passion for the sport but also a lifestyle. This is a team that can not only gather people but also bind them together—a team with a positive style of playing, based on leading the match. When FC Barcelona plays home games, there are always 100,000 spectators, and the event is so popular that season tickets are handed down through generations as an inheritance and are impossible to even purchase. Barcelona has its own soccer academy where most of the club's players come from. There, they learn the philosophy and thinking that manifests itself as such an integral part of the club's approach to sports. At the stadium, we surrendered to the force field created by the 100,000 hopeful spectators wearing the obligatory scarlet and blue colors. I have a small ritual with David, which consists of buying a bottle of water and a baguette with ibérico ham, at which point we are ready for the match.

Before the match started, David was tense—he was *so* nervous and testy that I had a hard time talking to him. At the half-time break, FC Barcelona was up by six goals—pretty much unheard of in soccer—he was on his toes and beside himself with excitement. Normally, when he sees his favorite team play he does not have any spare energy to eat or concentrate on anything but soccer. But with a lead of six goals, I nonetheless managed to persuade him to have a hot dog during the break.

I will conclude this book with a little story about David and his anticipation of what would happen in the second half and remind my readers that there is nothing more important than creating space in your life for looking forward to what will happen in the future. It does not have to be anything big or significant. It can be completely mundane things that you plan, because you have a feeling that what will happen at some point will give you that tickling sensation in your stomach. While I was still subject to the non-compete clause with Pandora, I was looking forward to the day it would expire. As I am ending this book, I am looking forward to meeting some of my friends tonight to have dinner at a good restaurant. Tomorrow morning I am looking forward to my meeting at 7:30 with an employee who is having some problems and needs to talk to someone who understands what he is going through. Later tomorrow, I am looking forward to going to Hamburg to meet some of my old friends. In the evening we will be going out to my old hunting grounds, EAST Hotel in Hamburg. The owner is an old friend of mine, and he already called to let me know that he had had my suite cleaned twice over because he knows how I feel about hotel rooms. So, tomorrow night I'm looking forward to a fantastic night out with some of the guys. We will start at the bar with cocktails and then have dinner in the hotel's restaurant. The owner is well aware that the restaurant is a little too fancy for my taste, so he will make sure to make his special meatballs that he knows I love so much. The hotel also has Hamburg's hottest nightclub and because the owner is our host, we will have our own place there were we can have fun into the early hours of the morning. I have told everyone I have met all week that that is what we are doing, and many of them have told me they will be there, too. It will be a mixed bag of people—some I know professionally and other are old friends I haven't had the time to connect with for a long time.

When I look forward to the future, I often do so in two very distinct ways. On the one hand, there is a type of joy in looking forward to creating a big business, reaching seemingly impossible goals, and breaking down barriers and conventions. On the other, I can experience joy in looking forward to the most everyday things. The energy of life is generated by an exchange between different states—between focused work and letting go, or between creating something big and being able to linger on very small things. If you forget either and just go full steam ahead to chase results constantly, life loses its glow. There is nothing more important than looking forward to change, to what you do not know will happen, or perhaps to the end of this book…and perhaps, hopefully, feel that some of what I have described in this book is something you can use in your life.

Jesper Nielsen

jespernielsen@endlessjewelry.eu

www.facebook.com/endlessjesper

IN CARSTEN'S WORDS

Postscript

With a book like this, a profile of a person with an exciting story to tell, I always hope to be able to tie up loose ends and perhaps clear up questions I have broached. To be sure, Jesper has raised a multitude of questions, shared his views on a myriad of topics, and told many different stories—we have woven these together, crisscrossing in various directions. We have rounded off some of the stories, but others have generated more questions than answers. It is too early to tell if Jesper will ever decide to resume his ambition to create the world's best sports team or what will happen with his case against the Danish tax authorities. And only the future will tell how fast Endless Jewelry will grow, when they will have specialty stores in all major cities, and—and I say this only half-tongue-in-cheek—when Jesper will finally make it to the moon and start selling Endless Jewelry there, too. The list of questions is long, and now that we know Jesper's fascination with endlessness and that he thrives on uncertainty—the list is bound to grow even longer over the next many years.

It may sound hackneyed but our work on this book gradually changed my outlook on life. If anyone had asked me before I met Jesper if I believed that a billion-dollar business could be built up around just letting your employees say "yes" to everything, aggressively cultivating openness and authenticity, working with your family, and trusting in people's fundamental goodness, I would have been highly skeptical. At the most personal level, meeting Jesper has shown me a unique, alternative and almost utopian way of growing through collaboration. Many of the people I know who have reached the global pinnacle within their fields have, like Jesper, a great implicit awareness of their abilities. When talking to them, one sometimes suspects that they might not quite be in control of things—but you feel their energy and sense that they possess a certain power with the capacity to generate pure magic. In fact, the general "energy"—for lack of a better word—which I have experienced in my sessions with Jesper has almost been more fascinating than the actual substance of his exploits and experiences. One of the most important things I have felt and realized through him is that money is not quite as rational a concept as my accountant stubbornly maintains it is. To me, there is no doubt that money has a spiritual dimension. Money is a measuring stick we use to quantify something that, in reality, is not measurable. Money represents expectations, dreams, hopes, and a lot of other inexpressible concepts. As far as money is concerned, Jesper displays an acceptance and boldness that is quite uncommon—he is not afraid of losing it and does not give much thought to how much money he has at any time. Anyone who can find that kind of balance in himself will always be able to attract money and will never lack anything materially. In many ways, Jesper's and my views of humanity are very similar, but when it comes to letting go of money our levels of confidence are very different. If there is anything I have taken away from our sessions, it is the ability and capacity to be generous. Still water has a tendency to become brackish and that, too, goes for finances. I learned about the importance of not being afraid of letting go of my money. For example, since I started my interviews with Jesper, I no longer regret or complain about unforeseen expenses; in fact, if I see a parking ticket on my windshield, I relax and just put it in my pocket. In terms of spending money, a ticket is the ultimate exercise in letting go and not clinging to your earthly possessions.

Jesper has an exciting life and meets all the criteria that we, as our culture, have been conditioned to recognize as hallmarks of success. Yet, I am also grateful that I am not in his shoes. Naturally, it is wonderful to be able to eat at some of the world's top restaurants, to travel and constantly meet new people, to drive the most expensive cars, to have your own jet, and to say and do whatever you feel like. However, if you live your life always pushing the envelope, it is not always easy to find time for quiet and reflection, to be yourself, to relate to what is completely down to earth or muse on a beautiful sunset. Contemplating sunsets is unlikely to be in Jesper Nielsen's cards in the near future. Out of all the people I have met, he is indisputably the person with the strongest work ethic. If I were not so laid back and uninterested in achieving business success, I would probably have both an inferiority complex and performance anxiety when he and I are together.

***

There is only a week left until we send Jesper's book to the printer, and I have just received an invite to visit him at his new headquarters in Düsseldorf, Germany. In order to no longer be at the mercy of the Danish tax authorities, the Nielsens finally decided to move their European headquarters to Germany. This will be their base as they develop the European component of Endless Jewelry over the next few years. The next day I find myself on a plane heading south. I rarely read newspapers, but I still take a paper when the air hostess offers me one on her way through the aisle. On the front page, there it is: an article about Jesper's tax case. I turn the page:

The tax authorities give Jesper Nielsen massive apology

The tax authorities have issued an official apology to businessman Jesper Nielsen for their months-long harassment of him and his family. In a ten-page letter sent to Nielsen's accountant, the tax authorities acknowledge that their treatment of Nielsen and his family has been "reprehensible," "unlawful," "completely unacceptable," "dismaying with respect to basic civil rights and due process," and characterized by "serious procedural issues," and that "Jesper Nielsen and his family have been subjected to completely improper pressure." The letter moreover notes that the Danish Internal Revenue Service "sincerely regrets these questionable matters related to the review of [your] case." Based on their review of the case, the tax authorities have decided to launch civil service proceedings against six Danish IRS employees, including a consultant who maintained primary responsibility for the review of Nielsen's case and who had drafted a number of explicit e-mailed threats to Nielsen's family.

"Well, we have obviously been vindicated with respect to many of the issues we've raised," Jesper Nielsen remarked to

the newspaper. "But an apology won't bring back our sports team and our loss of reputation throughout this prolonged nightmare. And apart from that, the tax authorities are still keeping my family and me in a vise. It goes like this: The IRS makes a mistake. Issues an apology. But then continues to tie up a large portion of my assets until it finally decides on what to do with my case. Now, we've no way of knowing how long they need to review this case. A number of highly-placed individuals at the IRS know they screwed up and they'll naturally do anything they can to keep this case in limbo. The day this case is finally adjudicated in court, these individuals know that they'll be held to account for their actions. Frankly, my trust and confidence in the Danish tax authorities is gone — I no longer wish to support the Danish state by conducting business in Denmark."

At Düsseldorf Airport, one of Jesper's staff members greets me and takes me out to one of the new Endless limos—a long white BMW with the Endless logo emblazoned on its side. After a brief drive, we arrive at Jesper's new luxury resort on the outskirts of Düsseldorf. In surroundings that resemble a botanical garden crossed with The White House, we sit down by the pool with a view of the garden. After our usual chit-chat about life in general, Jesper starts talking about his business.

"Endless Jewelry is currently running at what I'd call version 1.0. but we'll soon upgrade our business to run version 1.1. In other words, we're waiting in the wings with new versions of our products, websites, gift boxes, displays, commercials, and so on and so forth. Until now, Endless Jewelry has primarily been regarded as a German phenomenon, but as of January 1, 2014, it becomes a global phenomenon. As things stand right now, Endless is inarguably the most adroit and dynamic brand in the German market. We've rolled out our products to all the stores at an unprecedented rate. We've just completed our first round of road shows in Germany, introducing more than 400 new customers to our story and vision for Endless Jewelry. We're a very young brand, but as predicted, we're already being perceived as an integral part of the German jewelry industry. In Germany, we're therefore shifting gears and moving into phase 2, which is about creating a broader awareness of Endless Jewelry with our end consumers. In early March, we'll launch a massive national television campaign of the same order of magnitude as the one I once did for Pandora. We just sent our entire marketing department to Marrakech in Morocco to prepare that campaign and shoot some photos to illustrate our future vision of Endless Jewelry."

"You also just launched in the UK and Italy," I say "How are those efforts going?"

"In both countries, our sales teams have exceeded our expectations. During our first month of Endless's launch in Germany, we managed to get onto the shelves of no fewer than 38 stores. Our UK team bested that by getting Endless Jewelry into 47 stores during their first month. But their record was just beaten by our Italian sales reps who managed to get Endless Jewelry into 51 stores during the first month. That's a fantastic outcome—even more so because the three markets in Germany, the United Kingdom, and Italy are so very different. As we're sitting here right now, Endless Jewelry has made its way into nearly 1,000 stores in the first 10 months of its existence. Meanwhile, we're pumping resources into the United States where our level of ambition is as high as for *all* of Europe. At the speed we're going right now, within the next year, we'll be traded in nearly 3,000 stores all over the world. As at January 1, 2014, we're approaching 200 full-time sales reps in the field globally. Our launch plans for Switzerland, the Netherlands, and Belgium for the first months of 2014 are also in place. Our strategy is to keep the German market one step ahead of the others so that we can develop, test, and fine-tune our processes and then use those experiences to generate the same successes in the other countries. And what's more, the concept we've built up is so logical and easy to understand that our customers accept it almost immediately—they just get it!"

"But how are you going to make it grow that fast?" I ask "There have got to be some issues, no?"

"The only issue we've had so far is not being able to supply enough goods fast enough. Our customers are reordering at a breathtaking pace. But, as of today, we're all caught up and our customers have what they need for the holiday season. The last couple of weeks I've had to accept a role that's pretty unusual for me—to be able to supply enough items to the stores, I've actually had to ask my people to hold back a bit."

"But I take it your family's happy?"

"Yeah, and busy," Jesper says. "We're back in our favorite place. The old spirit is back and our family is back in its proper element. This past week, my father has been driving around Germany in his commercial van delivering jewelry packages to stores in some of the biggest cities. He absolutely loves taking part in reestablishing the kind of energy we had with Pandora back when we started up. It is just such a gift to be able to tap into the wonderful optimism that is evolving throughout our new Endless organization."

Jesper gets up and points to a sports car in front of the house.

"Today, you and I will make Düsseldorf ours. I'll show you our new Endless building at the absolutely best address in town. And then we'll eat at one of Germany's best restaurants, and before we go home, we are going to have a night on the town. But let's leave tonight out of the book, OK? Maybe one of your grandchildren will be able to pry that story out of you one day."

Jesper smiles as I get up. He knows perfectly well that I'm not exactly a party animal, but maybe I will enjoy myself anyway. Once in a while, I guess you need to sacrifice yourself for a good cause, do some research, and be a good ghostwriter.